T0208471

Soul-Time Therapy

A Time to Be Still and Connect with Soul

Charity Amy Murphy

BALBOA.
PRESS
A DIVISION OF HAY HOUSE

Copyright © 2018 Charity Amy Murphy.

Editor: Anna Bennett

All rights reserved. No part of this book may be used or reproduced by any means, graphic, electronic, or mechanical, including photocopying, recording, taping or by any information storage retrieval system without the written permission of the author except in the case of brief quotations embodied in critical articles and reviews.

Balboa Press books may be ordered through booksellers or by contacting:

Balboa Press
A Division of Hay House
1663 Liberty Drive
Bloomington, IN 47403
www.balboapress.com
1 (877) 407-4847

Because of the dynamic nature of the Internet, any web addresses or links contained in this book may have changed since publication and may no longer be valid. The views expressed in this work are solely those of the author and do not necessarily reflect the views of the publisher, and the publisher hereby disclaims any responsibility for them.

The author of this book does not dispense medical advice or prescribe the use of any technique as a form of treatment for physical, emotional, or medical problems without the advice of a physician, either directly or indirectly. The intent of the author is only to offer information of a general nature to help you in your quest for emotional and spiritual well-being. In the event you use any of the information in this book for yourself, which is your constitutional right, the author and the publisher assume no responsibility for your actions.

Any people depicted in stock imagery provided by Getty Images are models, and such images are being used for illustrative purposes only. Certain stock imagery © Getty Images.

Print information available on the last page.

ISBN: 978-1-9822-0899-8 (sc)
ISBN: 978-1-9822-0898-1 (hc)
ISBN: 978-1-9822-0900-1 (e)

Library of Congress Control Number: 2018908594

Balboa Press rev. date: 10/02/2018

AWARENESS

In all of life there is the capacity to become - Aware

CONTENTS

Excerpt: Your Soul is Ancient and Wise ix
Preface: How to Read this Book x

Part One

Chapter 1: A Question of Soul and a Bit about the
            Human Condition 1
Chapter 2: Living in Soul - Awaken to your True Self 10
Chapter 3: Getting A Sense of Self: Getting A Sense
            of Soul 20
Chapter 4: Going - in: Setting the Path for Recovery
            of Self 39
Chapter 5: Living our Dreams 52

Part Two

Chapter 6: Healing in Heart 69
Chapter 7: We are Energy - We are Light 92
Chapter 8: Healing in Body 109
Chapter 9: Family: Healing the Bonds that Brought
            Us Here 122
Chapter 10: Living in Spirit, Living in Soul 142
Epilogue: Seeing the New World 159

Appendix

Meditation: This Moment 163
Invocation: Prayer for a Healing World 165

Notes to Self 167

EXCERPT

Your Soul is Ancient and Wise

Your Soul is ancient and wise, and at its rawest it is who you are. It is what connects you and what sets you free. Living your life in Soul is coming back to your source. It is the living breath that keeps you going, it is the teacher within you, and if you listen to it with an open heart, you will hear it as it guides you through life and brings you back to yourself.

Slow down! See the signs and follow them! They will lead you back to yourself and towards your destiny. Your destiny is the life plan your Soul sets when and before it enters into this lifetime and it is full of life goals and life experiences that your Soul wishes to encounter so it can further grow in universal awareness and love.

Live now how you wish to live, be now how you dream to be. Heal your Heart, balance your Mind, free your Spirit and connect with the wisdom and knowing of your Soul.

By fostering compassion, beauty and joy in our lives we open to the essence of creation and can move forward with vision and peace in our hearts. Opening up to our Soul means opening up to our creativity and learning to bring joy to the world we live in.

The beauty of all creation lies within you. You
are a manifestation of your Soul-Self-Truth
experiencing the joyful expression of life.

HOW TO READ THIS BOOK

Some suggestions...

Take your time. Read slowly. Take breaks. Go for walks. Be in nature.

Throughout this journey I recommend that you keep a journal with you at all times. Your journal is to be your companion and confidante. Use it to write it all down, your thoughts, feelings, insights, questions, reflections, ideas, dreams, visions, guidance and whatever else is within you wanting to come out.

As well as working with the ideas and exercises put forth in each chapter, it is also important that you engage a dialogue with your *Higher Self* in discovering the *Truth* that lies within you. This will involve putting time aside each day for journal writing and reflection.

This practice will help you to build up your own sense of Self and start bringing your consciousness out for you to bear witness to. It is in this journey that you will begin to start being your own guide as to what it is you truly seek in your life, and furthermore how you are going to get there!

Daily Practice

Daily use of your journal can include the following:

❖ 1-3 pages of stream of consciousness writing.
❖ 1-3 affirmations to keep in your focus for the day.
❖ 1-3 wishes for yourself.
❖ 1-3 things you are grateful for in your life.
❖ 1-3 actions that you will commit to doing that day.

Also, take yourself out for a walk every single day, even if it is just for ten minutes, and use this time to allow your mind to rest and tap back into the beauty of life and all that is within you.

Your Spiritual Path

This is a book for all people of all faiths who are interested and commited to following their own spiritual path and allowing a space in which to connect with their own Soul. It is a book of inspiration and investigation into the greatness of the human spirit and it is a celebration of all that we are and all that we wish to become. This book will support you towards building a better life for yourself and the world you live in. This book will help you to change your life if you allow it to. This book is a book of healing, and by reading it you take your Soul on a journey home.

Take each step slowly and listen to your
Soul as you guide yourself home.

Namaste, Amen,
Charity Amy Murphy

Setting the Path

As YOU go on YOUR journey,

REMIND your Self of the core Values,

Of compassion
Understanding
Non-judgement

ALLOW your Self to sit in your Heart,

Connect with your Soul
Release negative Emotions
and limiting Thoughts

AFFIRM your Commitment to live your life in Awareness,

Love
Truth
and Beauty

REKINDLE your Joy for Life,

Open up your Curiosity
Engage your Mind
Fuel your Passion

And let YOUR Innocence return to YOU once more.

Part One

A Question of Soul and a Bit about the Human Condition

Step into your Soul and find your way back to yourself.
The beauty of all creation lies within you.
You are a manifestation of your Soul-Self-Truth
experiencing the joyful expression of life.

The Wisdom of the Soul Calls to Us

Each one of us holds within ourselves a wisdom that has not come from any book or been taught in any school. It is a wisdom of *Truth* and of *Knowing,* and it is held deep within us all.

All throughout our lives it constantly talks to us, guiding us on our journey - and if we will just stop and listen we will hear it as it guides us gently through our lives. If asked how we know, we answer – we simply *know.* In this state of being there is no logic, there is no explanation, there just *is,* and it is this *is,* that guides us throughout our lives and it is our *Soul.*

Stepping Out of Fear and Lack

Fear can hold us back from so much, and most of the time we don't even realize it. Fear stops us from really and truly being ourselves, from following our true path and from living from our hearts. It lives and breathes just like we do, because we allow it to exist in our world. We allow it to exist in our minds and in our own being.

Fear is a powerful energy that grows and spreads. It takes many forms and many disguises. It starts by entering our mind as a subtle doubt, and there it festers and grows, until one day we can find that it has come to consume us, trap us and control us. Fear of what to do, of who to be, fear of succeeding, fear of failure, fear of not being accepted, of not being loved, of not being liked, of not fitting in, of fitting in too much, of selling ourselves short, of choosing the wrong path, of choosing the right path, of not being understood. Fear, fear, so much fear.

Fear of this kind is an illusion of the ego-mind, a protective measure of limitation and separation learnt by the Self in absence of its connection to *Soul*. Its power for false truth pushes us to believe that it is real, and unfortunately over time we can learn to believe its false power and let it dictate our life choices. It can cause us to form walls around ourselves and even to block our own happiness.

We cannot allow fear of this kind to overwhelm us. It is a false low vibration that belongs to a part of ourselves that we have not yet come to understand and learn from. This part is our *Shadow Self* and it is full of learning and guidance. All we need to do, is start acknowledging it, seeing it and helping it to heal. Then the fear we have been holding gets to be dissolved, and we start living our lives from our true power, the power of our *Soul*.

This *Shadow Self* is very, very important. It will lead you through the path of your intimate being and it is crucial in helping you to move forward into who, as a *Soul* you really are, and to help you see the moments when you were shut off from yourself. The *Shadow* is a gift. It is your unconscious trying to gain your acceptance of who you are. Do not silence it, do not tell it to leave, for all you are doing is shutting a part of your Self off, a Self that needs listening to, a Self that feels it is unworthy to be. The disconnectedness we sometimes feel acts to throw us from our true path, our lifeline, our true essence, just remember we can get ourselves back on track just as quick.

We are always the one who holds the enlightenment into our own being.

So hold fast, all your emotions, both positive and negative. Let them work through your subconscious. We alone have the capacity to bring into our own consciousness the love and the light we choose to bring in. This is what is at our core truth. Feel it, allow yourself to honor your life. Allow your consciousness to open without ego, and honor your journey as you start to open yourself up to your Soul.

The Heart - Mind, Spirit - Soul Separation

The most common separation among people in contemporary society is with the heart and the mind. The growing emphasis on the hierarchy of the mind has led to the heart becoming something to be controlled, even denied. Placing such restrictions on matters of heart has led to people becoming disconnected, split and lost in themselves.

Sometimes this separation becomes so severe that the two parts learn to work in complete opposition to each other. The heart feels so much and the mind thinks so much, yet often each act in a state of not knowing what the other is doing, or why it is doing it. This not knowing often occurs with the two parts functioning at a level of impatient intolerance with the other.

Add to this the loss of a connection with Spirit and Soul and you find that it is no mystery that a lot of human beings live their lives in disharmony with themselves and their surroundings, being thrown from one state to the other, living their life in confusion and bewilderment at what they truly want, what will make and keep them happy, what they're doing with their lives and what they're not.

It is very important to know, and keep knowing that the Heart is the MOST powerful in all your interactions of life, all thoughts, all hopes, all fulfillment of you as a being of light. There is nothing higher than the heart and its essence can change worlds for the better.

Creating Harmony in Your Life

You cannot have harmony in your life if you do not have harmony in yourself. So even with the most basic level of separations you can find yourself living in a whirl of confusion, anguish, despair and conflict. And when in conflict, you are in battle. Only in this war - the enemy is yourself.

If this holds true for you, you will find you spend a lot of your life working against yourself, instead of for yourself, and this is simply because you do not know yourself in all your parts. You may have found that you followed certain paths only to discover at the end of them that they were not what you were really looking for.

You search for paths but really, what you are looking for is yourself and your own Truth. Life in all its joys and complexities teaches us how to disconnect. Not knowing how to reclaim ourselves we keep going forward in whatever direction we seem to be pointed, whether that direction is what we truly want or not, or whether it is what is truly best for us.

This is also true on a collective consciousness level and planetary level. Taking stock of ourselves and slowing down long enough to see, is the only way we can begin to step out and begin to create the life we truly desire and aspire to live.

Reclaiming Your Truth

So what's the answer? It's simple. Just stop. Stop battling with yourself, stop ignoring yourself and start listening. You and all your parts have all the answers. You can live your life blind, hiding from yourself, or you can choose to want to open your eyes and see. Going within, with Heart, gives your Soul air to breathe and unfolds your own divine wisdom so that you can heal yourself and follow your own unique guidance. Healing awakens Spirit and frees your mind to follow the journey of your Soul. We all have the power to create a heaven here on Earth. The first step is simply a stepping back, back into ourselves, and back into our Truth.

Connecting with Your Soul

In order to move yourself forward in your life you will in no doubt go through a time of shifting. During this time you will start to allow yourself to reflect on your life journey. You will also start to allow your curious nature to once again surface and begin asking questions of consciousness from your *Soul.*

Know that it is only by asking yourself questions can you ever hope to get to the answers that lie within you. So ask yourself and don't be afraid to hear the answers of *Truth* as they come back to you. Simply allow yourself to be open to your own inner wisdom and get to know yourself and all your greatness. Use your journal, do your daily practice and really begin to start being honest with yourself. This is your life and this is your journey, don't let yourself stay stuck. This is your time, a time for you to shine and grow, a time for you to get to know yourself. A time for you to let everything you couldn't say out loud out onto the pages for clearing. This is a time for you to heal and to claim your future for yourself.

Discovering A Want of Change

Discovering a want in yourself to change, heal and grow, can happen in many ways and at very different times in your life. Mostly people go through a process - a string of events brings a person to a conclusion and an acceptance of admitting to themselves that they have a desire of wanting to change. This process of wanting to change can happen many times before a person finally decides to take courage and face themselves.

It can happen slowly and gradually, until someday you find yourself picking up certain books or thinking differently about your life. Or, it can spiral out of a life-crisis. Just like every moment of every day holds a space in which you have the power of choice, every life-crisis brings with it an energy in which you have a chance to change the direction in which you are faced.

It is within this space that a gift dwells, a gift of time, a gift of reflection, and a gift of transformation.

Regardless of how you come here, this want of change always enters your life when you give it the space, and the chance to be. And for all, it is a time when you sense and know that somehow you want to be different. That your life needs changing, rearranging, growth, and you know that for this to happen it needs to come from within. You know that deep within your *Soul* you are not being completely true to yourself, and that life for you is lacking in some way.

You may feel that somewhere along the journey of life you have lost yourself and that as scary as facing yourself is, it is far scarier to face your future repeating the past and staying blind. You come at last to a place in your life where you want to discover who you really are and connect back fully with the beauty and essence of life.

You may not yet quite know how, or why your life has brought you to this place and that is okay, because your *Soul* does, and your *Spirit* does, and together with your *Mind* and your *Heart* you are going to figure it out; your way, and at your pace. You are the one in control and you sit in your Self by choice.

All you need do now is open yourself up to yourself, not just with your *Mind* or your *Heart*, but with your whole being. You want change; now give yourself permission to go where it takes you. Once you do that, all else will flow if you let it happen. Be gentle with yourself and slowly open your eyes, open your *Heart*, and allow yourself to get to know yourself once more.

The Gift of Choice

Choose to be true to youself, to listen to yourself and your dreams, and you will be filled with a life of peace and fullfillment. Stop chasing rainbows and find instead the rainbow inside your own heart. Let it shine out and touch all the hearts around you.

Choose to forgive yourself for the choices you are not proud of, let them go and bless them, for they allowed you to learn and they brought you through your experiences of life.

Forgive yourself, and in so doing understand we are all here doing the best we can, and we all have frailties of heart and aspects of ourselves that need healing.

The past is the past, the future is the future and the now is the *present*. Let your past go and learn from it. We have all done and acted in ways that we feel bad about at some point in our lives. We are also all capable of being true to ourselves and of going against ourselves, and we have this capacity every single second of every single day.

Sometimes we make good choices and sometimes not. The choices we make have a power in them, but they do not hold us for they are only choices and they can be changed at any moment. You can change how you choose at any moment and you can feel good knowing that you are the one with the power over your choices.

You can change your experience of life by changing how and what you choose. Choose to fill your life with love, beauty and joy and you will have a life experience filled with those qualities.

Know that people for the most part don't heal because they don't want to, they don't heal because they don't know how to, and it is fear of failure that often keeps a person locked into believing they don't possess the ability to change.

Have compassion for those that are stuck in old pain and ways of conditioning, and offer them a helping hand of grace for courage and change. Let them know that what we forget so often, is that we are magnificent beings with tremendous potential, and our power to transform and heal is profound.

People who are stuck, if they were really honest with themselves, would admit that yes they really do want change. They want all they dream of, they want love and they want healing, but they are so afraid that they wont get it, that it stops them from trying. Let's get rid of fear and let everyone know that, *Yes,* you can have all that is within your heart, you can heal, and you can be happy and whole.

All we need to do is take courage and begin the process of stepping back into ourselves and learn to open our inner guidance and our hearts to bring about the change and awareness we need to come into our lives.

If you can allow yourself to truly live in your own *Truth,* you will find your way back to yourself, and you will heal and you will become whole. Give yourself this time and begin to see your life as a means for growth and expansion. Start to embrace all your experiences, good and bad, positive and negative and look to see the lessons of *Soul.*

Everything in our life offers us a chance to learn more about who we are and come back into our hearts. It is only our association with our emotional and behavioral baggage that leads us to believe in a lack of love, a lack of *Soul* and a lack of plenty.

We play tricks with our hearts and our minds and we believe what we want to believe. So take this journey with an open heart and free yourself from fear and restriction. Start now, and slowly begin to look at your life and all your moments of growth. Let your *Soul* guide you - it will never lead you astray. It is your true north, follow it.

Journal time...

Take some time and think about an aspect from this chapter that stood out to you or resonated with you and write about it in your journal.

Exercise: Meditate for Five Minutes

Give yourself five minutes and meditate in silence and then write about your experience in your journal. See if you can do this every day for a week. And then expand it as you get more comfortable with it. Before you begin, either out loud or in your mind, say your full name. "I am..., I am my heart, I am my true heart." Then simply close your eyes and sit and be in your own energy.

Exercise: Practice Consciousness writing

This is an exercise in stream of consciousness writing: Take 10 minutes and write about anything that comes to you. Start the page by writing the day, date, time and place where you are and then just start writing. If you do this every day you will be amazed at how much starts to come out onto the page for you to uncover. You can set up a daily routine and do it with your morning coffee, or in bed before sleep or even on your lunch break. It's a really nice way to create a space in your day just for you and to have this time for yourself.

Chapter 2

Living in Soul - Awaken
to your True Self

Truth, Beauty, Innocence, Love.
Your Soul is Love, Your Soul is Understanding.
Your Soul is Beauty, Truth and Innocence,
because all doings of the Soul are held in
essence of God - Loving-Light-Energy

Slow Down See the Signs

Your Soul is ancient and wise, and at its rawest it is who you are.
It is what connects you and what sets you free. Living your life in
Soul is coming back to your Source. It is the living breath that
keeps you going, it is the teacher within you, and if you listen to
it with an open heart, you will hear it as it guides you through
life and brings you back to yourself.

Slow down! See the signs and follow them! They will lead
you back to yourself and towards your destiny. Your destiny is
the life plan your Soul sets when and before it enters into this
lifetime and it is full of life goals and life experiences that your
Soul wishes to encounter so it can further grow in universal
awareness and love.

All acts of the Soul are acts of love, they are pure and they
are free and they hold only support and love because they do
not come from mind, they do not come from ego and they do
not come from fear, they come from Source.

Quiet Contemplation - Sitting in Self

Learning to still the Self and connect with Source to live in consciousness is perhaps a daunting concept to imagine achieving, yet it is one of the simplest things you will do in this lifetime. All that need happen to allow its emergence is to slow down.

Stop rushing in your life and in your head. Stop filling your Self up with things you know you don't need or want. Cut through the layers of distraction and take control of You. Slowly allow your Self to let go of all the unnecessary fillers that you have devised over the years to act as a diversion to seeing yourself, and slowly and gently get to know yourself once more.

Your Soul knows what to do. It knows what lessons you have set yourself and it knows what joys await you. Your life here will work better if you work with yourself instead of against yourself. So let down the guards you have constructed around yourself and your ideas of life, and silently sit in your Soul, it will support you and comfort you if you let it.

In all your interactions start to bring a focus of awareness to them. For example: If you are in a conversation with someone, try becoming still and quite within yourself and consciously open up your awareness to really listen and hear what it is that this person is saying, give them your attention, see them, honor them, hear them, and be in the moment with them.

If you are cooking dinner, bring a quiet stillness to yourself and give the making of the meal your full focus. Enjoy preparing it, planning it and creating it. See the vegetables that grew in the earth so that you could nourish your body, so you could live, hold them - bless them, thank them. Think of the processes that occurred and the people who contributed their time and energy into bringing this food into your home and onto your table.

If you are driving - sit back, relax into yourself and enjoy the drive, slow down and connect with the motion of movement by letting yourself feel the joy and experience of driving. If you are playing with your children, then play with them and be with them fully, enjoy this time to be a child yourself, let go, have fun, be creative and let your imagination soar as you engage with the gift of innocence and love that children bring to our hearts.

If you are going for a walk then really go for a walk. Breathe in the fresh air and look at your surroundings, soak up the atmosphere of nature, of inspiration - look to the eyes of your fellow man and greet them, sharing your joy and enjoyment of being outdoors and moving amongst the world. If you are buying groceries in a shop see the person behind the checkout, smile at them, thank them, see them - honor them.

Begin slowly to allow yourself to be present in yourself in everything you do. Learn to be conscious of the tasks you are doing at the time you are doing them. Start to see and honor all the people you interact with, and remember to remind yourself to keep your conscious awareness open. Sit back, see, and experience all your moments.

Stepping Back in to See

Start by stepping back into yourself. Imagine going in and sitting down in your body. Get comfortable and sit further into yourself. Quieten your mind and all the internal chatter. Start to notice and catch your thoughts and still them. Sit in silence, be in silence and listen to it. Begin to see yourself in stillness and begin to see those around you in stillness. Sit within this space and allow yourself to be one with all that is and connect with the joy and beauty of life.

You can continue this throughout your day. Simply close your eyes and bring yourself into stillness. Imagine sitting into your body. Feel present. Feel peaceful. Start by putting a few minutes aside each day to connect with your Soul. Use this time to let your mind rest and tap back into the consciousness that is within each and every moment you have.

Remember you are Source, you are love and you are a part of the collective consciousness that we all live in on this planet, so take yourself seriously, and lightly let your *Self* play its part in this shared experience of life.

Soul Development

In the world of Soul, everything speaks to us. And just as in the time of the ancients, everything holds a deeper meaning and a sign towards Truth. The secret is to allow yourself to notice the messages that surround you and open your awareness so that you can decode the meaning that is there for you to uncover.

Begin by taking each day and all your daily experiences and look for the lessons of Soul that are there. Think back over your life. Can you think of any instances in your life that you feel you were being guided? This can be as simple as feeling strongly guided to go somewhere, do something or call someone - which if you followed, invariably led you on a happier, more fulfilled path.

Or perhaps there has been a time in your life where you found that when you tried to persevere in getting something - like for instance a particular new job, house, relationship, or college course - that you were constantly coming up against a brick wall, and that try as you may you just couldn't seem to make it work. Again this was a signpost trying to point you in a different, better direction. One that with hindsight, could just maybe lead you towards a happier more joyful life and perhaps turn out to be a much better fit for you.

Our lives are full of signposts from our Soul. When we slow down and begin to open up our awareness, we will see its presence more clearly as it guides us along our journey of life. Learn to see the signposts as you try to point yourself in the right direction. See everything as a signpost back to yourself. Learn with them and grow with them and start to open up your awareness.

Take a few moments and let yourself see if you can remember any of these signposts in your life. Write them down in your journal. When you are finished let them sit with you awhile and see if you can uncover what they were all about and where it was your Soul was guiding you to go.

Question to Find Truth

Question, Question, Question... And find your own Truth. Unravel all thought forms until you get to its purest essence, its Truth. Question until the Truth in you recognizes the Truth in it, and you become one with that Truth and the Truth of all that is. Everything we need to know we already know. All your answers are inside you. Writing and journaling is a great way to tap into your inner Self and often if let flow, acts as a channel for your Soul to be heard.

Write down a question and let the answer come from deep inside you. Meditate on your questions, stay with them. Allow them to resonate inside you and the answers will come to the surface when they, and you, are ready to let them out and be heard.

Everything that comes to us comes when we give it the space and the time to be. Allow your mind to free itself. Allow your thoughts to shift and change, be open to differing beliefs. Old ways of identifying oneself by way of one's beliefs is being replaced by Spirits desire to experience freedom, and this can only come about if you unlock the prison you have formed around your mind. Go back and unlock the door and then unchain the thought forms that you have created around certain ideas of life and being.

Questions of Soul:

What do you, me, we, us, want out of our lives?
What are the things that matter most to us in life?
What are the most precious experiences we can have in life?
What will be our legacy to the world, individually and collectively?
How can we hope to live this lifetime and enrich the world around us?

Ask yourself:
What is my Truth?
What do I want to accomplish?

What do I hope to share?
What do I hope to teach?
What do I hope to give?
What do I hope to leave after I move on?
What do I hope to learn while I'm still here?

Your beliefs:
What do you think they are all about?
Where have they come from?
Why do you believe them?
Who started them and why?
What is their Truth?
What is their Essence?

My Reality - Right Here - Right Now

Take a moment here to clear your mind by taking a few deep breaths, relax into yourself and get rid of clutter. Be real with yourself and look around you. Where are you? Really look. See what is in front of you. What are you being shown or directed through circumstance to develop within?

Where are you right now? What is your reality? Where have you brought yourself? Who is in your life? What do you do with your time? What is your profession? What are your pastimes? Where do you live? Who are your friends? Who is your lover/ your partner/your spouse? Who are your family? What lessons do you think are here, right now, in your now, for you to learn? Where is your joy, your laughter, your lightness?

Where is the love in your life? Who opens your heart and fills it with joy? Who in your life do you think you may be using to reflect aspects of yourself back to yourself? What are they trying to teach you? What are you trying to teach you through them? Where is your heart, are you in it? Do you know it? Have you healed it? Can you bless it? Can you share it? Can you love it?

Everyone is a mirror. Our whole reality is a mirror. Our outward experiences showing us a reflection of our inner self.

Step back from yourself and look into your mirror. Let your ego go and step into the *Truth* of your heart. Heal all aspects of yourself that need healing, including your relationships. Forgive, release and let go. Step into your Soul and find your way back to yourself.

Use all your relationships as a tool for reflection. How healthy are they? Can you see the love in them? The kindness, the respect? Is it a two-way street? Both giving and receiving, nurturing and loving. Take a good look at friendships, family, partners, and then with reflection and your own honesty allow yourself to see the truth in them. Do they match you in vibration? Is there room for growth, expansion, connection?

Heal, grow and transcend through any and all forms of negativity and limitation until you see the love and the truth that lies beneath and within every experience you have. If you find that some relationships are unhealthy then don't be afraid to take time to ascertain if it is for your highest good. Meditate on it and see if it is within your power to bring healing to it, or do you need to allow the other to ascertain their responsibility in it. Learn to see with eyes of love. Learn to heal your past and learn to hold a heart of compassion and understanding for those around you and for yourself. Learn to face yourself and come back into your heart and let your *True-Self* shine through.

The Peaceful Power of Gratitude

A big part of living in *Soul* is learning to see, experience and give thanks for all that is good and precious in our lives. Sometimes in the hustle and bustle of life we forget to dwell on the good that exists in our world. We become so focused on what we feel is missing and what we believe we need to get or have, that we forget to focus on what we already have.

Having a sense of gratitude in our lives can greatly improve our quality of life and also help remind us of the joy that exists within us and others. Being grateful is the art of being able to slow down within ourselves so that we can look around us and give thanks for all that we are, all that we feel, all that we experience and all that already is.

It is about learning to change our outlook in our everyday experiences, even if just for short amounts of time and start noticing and celebrating the small things that we can see. Gratitude is an affirmation of goodness from our heart out to the world. When we are able to be grateful we begin to notice that our life is full of precious gifts. Like everything, it takes practice.

The more we practice being grateful the more grateful we will become. The more grateful we become, the more grateful we will be. Gratitude celebrates life and everything in it. Noticing and appreciating others affirms our connection to one-another and helps us all to see our world in a brighter and lighter way. Gratitude is everywhere we choose to look. We can see it, feel it and experience it, in our communities, our homes, our work and our relationships.

Start looking around you and see the life that exists alongside you, see the flowers, the birds, the people, the things people have built and created that you have been fortunate to be witness to.

Learn to be grateful for and give focus to what you have, not what you don't, and learn to bring this into your consciousness for celebration and for thanks. Take a few minutes each day and stop and think about the love, beauty and friendships that you have in your life. List your findings in your journal and see if you can add three to it each day.

Time is Life

There is so much time put into confusion in this life that sometimes, it, life, just gets passed by. No time to take notice, time passes by and we have to keep up. Got to keep moving, things to do, very important, can't stop, quick, move out of my way, I'm busy, very busy. I'm so busy I'm forgetting to live my life. I'm forgetting to see my life, to experience my life, to love my life, to share my life, to know my life. I'm so busy I don't even know what my life is anymore, what am I doing, where am I going?

The importance of time lies in the *Now*. Every minute and every second is the now. It is now - Now. Time is not just hours and minutes but is in fact, our lives. So when we misuse time or let it dictate, we are in fact misusing our lives. When we let our assumptions of time interfere and confuse us we are allowing an illusion to enter into our psyche as a form of limitation.

Live now, the way you want to live. Be now, the way you dream to be. Time has no existence except in the Now. You came here to experience the capacity to feel love and the capacity to give love and to intertwine the two in your being and in your life, so experience it now – it's time!

At the end of the day this is all time - The question is what do you want to be doing with your time? Time is life. How you spend your time is how you spend your life. Think about the values and qualities of life that are important to you, think about the type of person you want to be and then keep moving yourself forward in yourself and in your life. Remember to give thanks regularly and bless everyone and everything in your life including yourself. Love everyone and everything in your life including yourself.

Heal all relationships, they are all a part of your story and thus a part of you. Learn to bring all your daily encounters into your life for honest reflection of you back to you and start creating a life you truly love. A life of connection, a life of love, a life of beauty, a life of joy.

Journal time…

Take some time and think about an aspect from this chapter that stood out to you or resonated with you and write about it in your journal.

Exercise: Signposts from My Soul

Take a few minutes now and in your journal make a list of the signposts of Soul that have stood out to you so far in your life. See how many you can remember and then write it all down. Then relax into yourself and objectively allow yourself to see if your Soul is showing you signs right now to help you to grow.

Signposts from my Soul...

Exercise: My Gratitude List

Think about 10 things you are grateful for in your life. See if you can add three to it each day and keep a record of them in your journal.

I am grateful for...

Chapter 3

Getting A Sense of Self:
Getting A Sense of Soul

The only true tragedy of one's life
is the un-recognition of one's Soul.
The embodiment of life is the
embodiment of the Soul into form.

Soul Evolution

Basically what we are all doing here on this wonderful planet we call Earth, is evolving as Souls. Every person on this planet is a manifestation of their *Soul* and each person is experiencing the journey their Soul chose to experience so that they could heal and grow in conscious awareness. All change comes from raising our consciousness and that means being honest with ourselves and all our experiences that we have had along our journey of life.

We are all here for the same reason and we are all the same, the only difference that exists, is how we navigate our way through the experiences of life. Your whole life has led you to this moment, to begin the next chapter in growth, understanding, joy and *Truth*. To move, shift and evolve into who you really are - a perfect manifestation of *Spirit* and *Soul*, brought to Earth to learn, to share and to love.

All our experiences throughout our lives are ours to grow with, and all act as a gauge back to ourselves. Each helping us to grow and develop our psyche. To mature with conscious awareness, resilience and increasing capacity to lead our own lives.

A Time for Healing

Life Mapping and Reflection work is a way for you to discover a *Sense of Self* and from that a *Sense of Soul*. It is a personal journey of discovery and awareness, from which you can begin to see where you have brought yourself in life.

It is a place in which you can start to see your life through the eyes of your *True Self,* your Soul, thereby allowing you to heal wounds from your past and free yourself so that you can live your life, knowing yourself, not from the mind of the ego but from the heart of your Soul.

All our experiences make up who we become. Doing a short synopsis of the significant events in your life will firstly help to jog your memory of those past events, and secondly help you to look at your life from an overall perspective.

Part One: The Sum of All My Parts - Significant Events

Events to include in your Life Map are: What type of birth you had, any childhood memories that are strong for you, changes within your family, the birth of your siblings, starting school, meeting close friends, any illnesses, accidents or operations, moments of achievements, your first love, the start and/ or end of significant relationships, emotional upsets, times of trauma or crisis, your first job and any or all jobs after, your first home, moving house, travelling, Any learning or courses you took, getting married, the birth of your children, nephew, nieces, the birth of your grandchildren, the death of loved ones, and any moment in your life that is significant for you. When you are finished filling in your life map take your time to read through it, reminding and reminiscing on the journey you have taken so far in your life. If you need extra space please use a separate sheet or continue within your journal.

Life Map

Getting a *Sense of Self* - Getting a *Sense of Soul*

Year	Age	Significant Event	Significant Event	Notes/ Reflections of Growth

Year	Age	Significant Event	Significant Event	Notes/ Reflections of Growth

Year	Age	Significant Event	Significant Event	Notes/ Reflections of Growth

To Thy Own Self Be True

If you are true to yourself you can never go wrong, right? Right! Then how do so many people go through life in turmoil, upset, confusion, hurt, anger, disappointment, regret...? Because they think they are being true to themselves when in fact they don't even know what their *Self* is anymore. They find themselves reacting to series of events and encounters, playing out programs, interacting, deciding and living out a life that they feel powerless to control. You have power over your life. No one else.

What about all the "stuff" that's "happened" to you. All the pain, the hurt, the obstacles, the hardships. From birth to childhood, from adolescence to adulthood, all along the way we are constantly transforming and growing.

Growing up is one of the most powerful transformations we make in life. It is glorious and challenging, and completely open to experiences of all kinds. It is in this vortex of discovery that we learn who we are, and who or what other people want us to be.

It is a time when we change and alter ourselves, sometimes out of a natural growth and development, and sometimes out of a want to be accepted. This is also a time when we first start to seek and determine a sense of independence and control over our lives.

All our experiences throughout our lives act as a gauge back to ourselves. As human beings we constantly strive to find ways to mark ourselves out, by consciously and unconsciously seeking out situations and experiences that specifically act to shift our transition within ourselves and mark our own growth. We continually seek and mark, from infant to adolescent, from adolescent to young adult, and so on and on we go continuing this cycle throughout our lives.

Constantly we seek and we mark, we seek and we mark, over and over again. The truth is, we never stop growing up. We are all on a continuing journey of growth and development, and we all consistently seek out and mark areas of our lives, and of our "selves," so that we can gauge our own self-worth and see how we are doing.

Your Life Map is your space in which to look back and see where you were seeking and marking your areas of growth. It further gives you the space to take back your power by stepping back into yourself, so you can now consciously lead the development of your future experiences.

The Experience of Life

We come into this life to learn and to grow and to connect. Experience is what allows us to do that. We come here to know, and each and every experience we have brings us there.

Think back to a hard or significant time in your life. Think about who you were before that experience. Now think about who you were after it. Had you changed? Did you grow, did you learn? Did it act to shift you in some way? Its emergence in your life is there for you to grow from. If you haven't gone in and healed it, and learned from it, then you still can. This is the beauty of looking at our lives from our Soul, for it offers us a deeper perspective, a path towards wholeness that does not exist in the eyes of the ego.

Embracing your experiences as tools to your own personal growth is taking back your power. They are experiences; they are tools to your own fulfilment of living a human life. It is a rich life, full of possibilities and encounters, and it is one of expansion. You are not meant to stay small and protected, you are meant to stretch out and fulfill your destiny. Extend out, experience, learn, heal, share and grow.

Part Two: Getting a Sense of Soul - Reflections of Growth

Getting a Sense of Soul is the second part in your Life Map. This is a time for you to sit back and look at your past life experiences by looking at the journey you have taken from the *eyes of your Soul.* See if you can figure out the lessons you have set yourself and if you can glimpse your areas of growth and markers of change along your journey of life.

In all our experiences we are learning and seeking out areas of growth for ourselves. Each and every experience holds a deeper truth and lesson for our *Soul.* Look and see where your areas of growth and learning are, and see if you can discover what you are trying to tell or teach yourself.

See the moments and times in your life when you got to confront and witness your shadow *Self,* the *Self* beneath the one you show to the world, the one that is vulnerable, hurting, exiled, forbidden or forgotten, and see if you are able to embrace it and bring it into your heart for acceptance, healing and love.

Go back to your life map and in the section **Notes/Reflections of Growth,** think about how you were before the *significant event,* how you were after it, and mark down in the space provided, what it meant to you, how you grew from it, how it challenged you, how it helped you, what it brought up for you or what it was pushing you to learn. It can be just a word or a sentence but let it signify the lesson or reflection of growth that you feel you received. Use your journal for exploration.

Soul-Time Therapy - The 10 Key Questions to ask Yourself:

1. How was I before this event?

2. How did this event affect me, if at all?

3. How did this experience help me to grow?

4. Am I still learning from this experience?

5. In what way did I grow from this experience?

6. In what way can I grow from this experience?

7. What shifts occurred within me from this experience?

8. Do I need to let go of any pain from this experience?

9. How did my heart open or close because of this experience?

10. What awareness, acceptance, releasing is left for me to do with this experience?

Use these 10 key questions to reflect on all your *significant events* that have stood out to you in life and also new ones that emerge along the way. Some answers will jump out at you like bolts of lightning coming straight into your consciousness. Others will need patience and time to surface.

I have always found that actually writing down the question on paper channels my mind and consciousness, to allow the truth of that experience to come from the depths of my Soul out onto the page for me, to sometimes bear witness to for the first time. Try it and see if that works for you. Carry your journal around with you, as you will be surprised when insights reveal themselves to you.

It is a very exciting time for you and it is something that you need to do at your own pace: it could take hours, days, weeks or even months. There is no rush. It is a healing process, an awareness opening process, and a space for truth and light to come through, so give it the space to be.

Patience and kindness to your own *Self* are very important through this journey, and you may want to have a trusted partner or therapist to talk through things with. Alternatively, you may be happy to do it solo, taking it in your stride and seeking a more solitary inward private development. Again, do what works for you; the great thing about this is that it will be different for all of us because we are all different. Just be wise enough to seek support if you are finding you need to. The power of talking with someone is tremendous and in itself can offer a healing space and a place for growth and compassion, so follow your path with this in mind.

The Power of Responsibility for Self

Many of us live our lives believing that external factors shape our lives. That we are somehow dependent on the structures that surround us, be they family, society, culture, economics, politics, sex, or race. Often we lose the reality of what we want, based on what we believe we can have, or what we believe we deserve. We forget that we are the ones who shape our lives, and that we alone are responsible for the quality of life we live.

Taking responsibility for your life is sometimes hard to do if looked at solely from the ego mind. Yet ironically this is the role that the majority of us are thought to believe in. Looking at your life through this filter acts to put past pain and life experiences into a false sense of unbearableness and fear, and further pushes us to see our future possibilities as battles to win or lose. It is this fear that leads us to look at our lives from a limited perspective and hides us from the truth of our true selves.

When you can take stock and look at your life from your *Soul Self*, you will discover that you can embrace all your life as an experience in energy, love and awareness. You will see that taking back your role of *Responsibility for Self* is the most freeing of actions that you will encounter in your life. We are more than our fears and we are more than our experiences, we are *Soulful* beings on a life experience, experience being the operative word.

It can be a weird sensation to realize looking back at your life, how you might have lived some of it in hiding, not knowing who you truly were or what you were doing. It can be scary and confusing, but it is also tremendously brave and courageous and once taken catapults you into your future and into your *Now.*

With new found awareness and perspective you may ask yourself: how was I not aware then? How did I do the things I did? Why did I follow that path? Why did I make that decision? You may see moments when your authentic *Self* tried to step through the tangled events that you brought yourself to and through.

You may see how there have been times when you have dared to step out, and you may also see the times when you have remained hidden. You may come to admit to yourself finally that a lot of your life was spent going through hoops, some your own, some others.

Jumping through without even a thought on what was in the hoop, who was holding it, or who it belonged to, and most the time not even stopping long enough to see if you really wanted to jump through the hoop in the first place.

The act of *Self Realization* is a fundamental step forward on your path of taking back your power and facing your life, and as you grow in courage and awareness along this path, you will realize that everything that you thought you couldn't face loses its grasp on you. It is here you begin to really break down any strands of fear that are in your subconscious and bring them out into the light. Out of the shadows for you to release and let go of, free to be who you truly are.

As you shift through the steps along this journey you will feel the denser, heavy energy that once surrounded you at times of difficulty take on a lighter brighter air. Life becomes something to live and experiences become something to welcome.

The Movie of Life

Try thinking of your life as a movie and you are an actor playing out the role you have been given. This role involves you getting to know your personality and character. You also have to accustom yourself with your character's background. Who are their family and friends? What has been their life experience? What are their dreams and aspirations in life? What obstacles do they have to overcome? What is their story? What is their Now?

Now imagine you are the writer of this movie. What is the story about? How have you planned the development of the story? What are the plot points and obstacles marked along the way for your character to overcome? How does your character handle them? What is the journey you want your character to go through? Who are the supporting actors in the movie? And how do all the characters come together to give meaning to each other's story? What is their relationship to one another, and to you?

Now imagine you are the director of the movie. What way do you instruct your actor to interpret the story and play their part? How do you guide them through the development of their character? How do you support them? What advice do you give them? Where is the story taking them?

This is how life works - Our *Soul-Self* is the writer of our script. Our *ego* and *Higher Self* plays the part of the respective actor depending on which part of ourselves we are choosing to act from, and our *Spirit* is the director. From a Soul level we pick personality and character, we choose family, friends and Soul mates, we select plot points and we determine dreams and aspirations. Then we come down to Earth and we start acting out our role as we have designed it.

We Write it, We Direct it and We Star in it

Some of us are not aware that we wrote "our movie" and we think we are just actors playing out the script that has been given to us. Some know well, and work hard at tweaking their scripts to reflect their learning as they grow in conscious awareness.

When we slow down and start connecting with our *Soul-Self* we can begin to see the story we have written for ourselves. When we begin to see, we can begin to learn and grow. From this we can start to unfold our own *Truth* and start to direct ourselves in conscious awareness and development. Tapping back into ourselves allows us to tap back into the consciousness of all existence for that is our truest state and where we come from. Learning from our experiences of life enables us to open ourselves up to this consciousness and live our lives from our *Higher or Highest-Self.* Then we can move forward in true awareness, true harmony and true intention.

Part Three: Soul View: On Reflection - Getting a Sense of Soul in my Life

This is the part where you get to write it all down and release anything and everything that needs to be released at this time. Use this space to allow yourself to take in all that you have done, been, seen and experienced so far in your life and write down what you feel your life experience is showing you.

Look back over your Life Map, significant events and reflections for growth and see what experiences stand out to you. Then write down what needs to be healed, what you need to let go of, and what you feel you have learned and grown from.

See also if you can get a sense of your *Soul* in it all, and if so, what you think it is trying to tell you, or teach you. Take your time and allow yourself to look to your heart for guidance.

Charity Amy Murphy

Use the space provided in the exercise: Notes to Myself, or if you prefer record your writing in the pages of your journal.

Exercise: Notes to Myself:

Reflecting on my life and all my experiences, I now can see how my Soul...

_____

_____

_____

_____

_____

_____

_____

_____

_____

_____

_____

_____

_____

_____

_____

_____

_____

_____

_____

_____

_____

_____

_____

_____

_____

_____

_____

Charity Amy Murphy

_____

_____

_____

_____

_____

_____

_____

_____

_____

_____

_____

_____

_____

_____

_____

_____

_____

_____

_____

_____

_____

_____

_____

If you need extra space please continue on a separate sheet or within your journal.

When you are finished take a break and let everything sit with you a while as you contemplate your life, the choices you have made, the paths you have followed, the turns you have taken and the destinations you ended up.

In all look to discover the love that is present in your life and the *Soul* lesson that resides in the experience you had. Look at the path you have taken, look at the signposts that your *Soul* placed down for you to notice, to direct you.

Look to your *heart* and know that everything that comes to us in life is fundamentally marked out for our *Souls* growth and your highest good.

Affirmation: The Truth of my Soul guides
me as I make my journey in life.

The Healing Process

Healing oneself is very much a process, and this process involves you connecting with yourself and the world around you in a non-judgemental and compassionate way. Its journey begins on a want to be healed, a desire and a need for change, and a conviction of moving from a state of limitation to a state of *Truth*.

This process is your process. You lead it, you are the healer and the healee. You are the miracle worker, the transformer. You are the light that shines through to show you where to go and how to do it. All you need to do is talk to that *You*, the one you left behind, the *You* that knows.

This process, as rewarding as it will be, won't always be easy and there will be times when you will need to take a break and switch off. This is healthy if kept in balance with your overall *Soul* journey. Switching *off* a lot of the time offers a space for the inner deeper reflection that is going on without your conscious awareness.

If you can start with a mindset of opening up your awareness as a purely experimental exercise, then you can begin to enjoy the journey as an adventure in which you are the explorer on a quest for hidden treasure. Keep in your own light and remember that it will not always be easy to go through, because at these times you will often be consumed with the pain, grief, confusion and anger that often comes with something worth going through.

These feelings of confusion, pain and possibly anger can sometimes overwhelm us and we will want desperately for them to go away; "*if only we can take control of them, stop them and make them disappear.*" Your focus in these moments will most likely be on the immediate and on trying to figure a way out, or a solution to the problem at hand. Our first reaction is always to try to "fix" the problem, mend it somehow, when really it is ourselves we need to fix and mend.

If we can refrain from our first impulse to just simply "fix" the problem and make it go away, and instead can allow ourselves to sit into it for a while and reflect on its manifestation into our life as something to grow from, then we can begin to see why it has come into our lives and, further, what it is our *Soul* is asking us to learn, heal or develop within ourselves.

Whichever and whatever way you choose to take your journey, remember that all you really need to do is to sit into your experiences and converse with your *Soul*. Opening up to *honest reflection* allows truth to come through the fog of our conditioning. This clearing opens up a space where the sun can illuminate our path and we find that we are no longer walking in our own darkness but in our own light.

Be honest with yourself when you can be, and see what comes from it. It can cast new light on old beliefs and help you see where you have been coming from.

Allowing yourself to heal means moving yourself forward and being the creative power in your own life. It is not blame it is consciousness. Let the past go and move yourself forward in your story of life.

By taking this step you choose to stand out of the darkenss and into the light of your own being. Journeying in allows you to see where you have been, so that you can now choose where it is you want to go. Take each step slowly and listen to yourself as you guide yourself home. Connect fully with your *Soul-Self-Truth* and take your journey back out into the Universe and into your heart, where it all began.

Journal time...

Take some time and think about an aspect from this chapter that stood out to you or resonated with you and write about it in your journal.

Exercise: The Time Line of My Life - My Precious Moments

It can be a nice idea to create a timeline of your life, celebrating all of your fondest and most precious moments and significant events. You can be as creative with this as you like. Try adding photos or sketching places, people and events. You could also use newspaper archives or add in some of your favorite or memorable song lyrics, poems, or sayings. Have fun and make it a collection of all your fondest and most precious moments in life, a true celebration of all you have loved so far in life.

My Precious Moments:

Going - in: Setting the Path for Recovery of Self

The Truth of your Soul speaks to you.
It gently whispers in your ear
and guides you through your life.

The Law of Attraction and Your Highest Good

The law of attraction works with energy and vibration. This means that we can draw towards ourselves what we want and need to come into our lives at specific moments in time by simply aligning ourselves in clear and conscious ways. When our wants and needs are in accordance with our own divine plan and higher good then life takes on a harmonious joyful flow. However, when they are not in line with our higher selves then, they (our wants, and needs) can bring to us negative attractions that we have unwittingly sent out into the Universe.

The law of attraction is about energy, and energy signals. Like energy attracts like energy. Just like magnets pull and push against each other so to do our thoughts, feelings, unconscious and conscious minds. Attraction is the purest of the forces of nature and it is what holds our world in order. If we can learn to use it for our highest good, then we can learn to live more authentic and abundant lives.

The secret to manifesting with the *law of attraction* is to be coming from a sense of alignment within yourself. In other words, for you and all your parts to be wanting and needing the same thing, and for those things to be what is best for your highest good.

This goes for Heart, Mind, Spirit, Soul and Body. If any one of those parts in you is not in alignment with the want and need you are sending out to the universe then the attraction has difficulty coming to you because you are inadvertently giving out mixed signals to the universe.

Not being in balance with yourself also causes confusion both internally and externally and can lead to depression, anxiety and feelings of being lost and confused in yourself and in your life. Tapping back into our own knowing is what unlocks the door back into our *Soul* and brings us once again to connect with our own *Truth*.

Connecting and Communicating with Self

This next step involves you talking directly to your Heart, your Mind, your Spirit, your Soul and your Body, so that you can see where you are in your life, and further to see what you are needing to give to yourself. It is all about finding out just how you are doing, not just on the surface, but deep within, and then applying what you have learned to bring balance and harmony into your life.

Doing this helps you to become healthy, whole and complete. It is also a blueprint for discovering where and what you need to heal, and learn how to start working with the law of attraction to manifest your true needs and desires in life.

Going in is your compass, your teacher and your guide. It is a way to discover what it is you are searching for, what you may be lacking, what it is you truly need or desire, what it is you feel, and how you can learn to be whole. It is all about learning to listen to ourselves and all of our parts as they tell us what we need to hear. They know the answers and if we are willing to step out of their way, they will tell us. Then we can start manifesting the life we want, in harmony and balance with our inner selves.

By following and honoring your inner guidance, you will come to bring a sense of harmony into your now and into your future. From this all abundance can flow through you, and you can begin to attract healthy opportunities into your life. Coming from a state of alignment within also means you will naturally start to work in *harmony* with *the law of attraction* and begin manifesting positive life choices that will help you to move forward more freely in your life.

We all hold the key to our own happiness, "going in" is the only way you will know how you are really doing on the inside, and by opening up to *honest reflection* you will give yourself the space in which to realign yourself with your *True Self* and your highest good.

Exercise: Going in for Guidance - Heart, Mind, Spirit, Soul, Body

The best way to know how we are doing is quite simply to ask ourselves. Use the guidance that comes up from the next few exercises to bring balance back into your Self and therefore into your life. Then start manifesting your desires of Heart, Mind, Spirit, Soul and Body in unison, to bring about a life you truly aspire to live.

If, along your journey of life, you come up against things that you are not quite sure about, or you sense you are losing touch with where you're going, then take out this exercise and use it to tap back in with yourself.

All you have to do is sit quietly and allow yourself to "go in" and ask yourself and all your parts how they are doing. Then, use the power of intention to manifest the true desires that lie within you. Hold space with your *Truth*, give it space to be, and allow it to take form into your life and into your consciousness.

What is going to come up for you is guidance, they are your parts, they are all a part of you - they are you. Learning to connect and know them helps you to hear them as they serve to guide you, as you serve to guide you. For the only person who really knows you is you, and the only person who really knows what you need, wish, dream and feel is you. So follow and know your own guidance and learn to trust in yourself, and in your own abilities as you guide yourself through your life.

Before you start, have a pen and paper beside you to write what comes up. This is your first step in connecting and communicating with yourself and all your parts. Be gentle with yourself and allow yourself to find out just how you are really doing on the inside.

Meditation: Going into Self

Before you begin, find a quiet place where you will not be disturbed. Get comfortable and give yourself this moment to just be in the presence of your own Self.

Grounding and Centering Breath Work

Take a minute or two to ground and center yourself. Sit up tall, stand straight or lie flat on the floor. Close your eyes and join your thumb and index fingers together.

Now take in a deep, long, slow even breath, filling up your belly, feel the breath fill your body and extend your rib cage out as you breathe in. Hold for a count of 5. 1... 2... 3... 4... 5, then breathe out slowly and steadily flattening your stomach in fully pulling it in and up. Do this two more times and each time I want you to imagine your *Self* being more and more in your *Body*. Breathe in and hold for 1... 2... 3... 4... 5..., breathe out, breathe in and hold for 1... 2... 3... 4... 5..., breathe out. Let each breath relax your *mind* and ease all tension away. Sit in yourself and feel whole. Continue to breathe gently in... and out..., in and out..., slowly and gently, in... and out...

Start by Visualizing Yourself as you are right now. See and feel yourself sitting in your *Body*, feel whole, feel present. Now picture your *Heart* in the center of your being, hold space with it and acknowledge it.

Now picture your *Mind*, feel its strength and beauty. Now picture your *Spirit*, like a bright shining light beaming out of you, sense its presence in you and feel it giving life energy to your *Heart*, your *Mind* and your *Body*. Breathe in and feel with every breath the light of your *Spirit* shining brighter and brighter, illuminating in and all around you.

Now picture your *Soul*, feel its wisdom, its knowing and its love. Hold space and breathe deeply and gently, feeling a connection with all your parts.

This is You.

Going - in: Heart – Mind – Spirit – Soul - Body - How are we doing?

Pick up your pen, stay still and quiet and continue breathing gently and stay centered in your own space. Be completely open with yourself and let whatever wants to come out, out. Your pen is their voice, so let them speak through you out on to the page.

You may be shocked at the honesty in which your parts talk to you, or you may know already what they are going to say. Do not judge them or yourself and hold yourself in a complete place of love. Remember, be open and honest, no one is judging you - not even yourself. Really connect with yourself and ask each of your parts in turn the question - how are you doing? Then simply begin answering, letting their knowing flow out of you onto the page.

And so, begin...

My Heart is...

_____

_____

_____

_____

_____

My Mind is...

_____

_____

_____

_____

_____

My Spirit is...

_____

_____

_____

_____

_____

My Soul is...

_____

_____

_____

_____

_____

My Body is...

_____

_____

_____

_____

_____

Charity Amy Murphy

When you are finished take a moment to relax and then read what you have just written and absorb it. You have just talked directly with all your parts and they with you. Thank them and hold space for a while. When ready, continue on.

Exercise: Honoring My True Self

Looking back on what came out of your going - in session, what sort of things came up for you? How do you feel reading what you wrote? Were you surprised? Were you honest? Can you stay honest? Will you use what you have learned to move yourself forward, to complete healing, to let go of what is no longer needed. Now that you have started the process of getting to know yourself - will you stay true to yourself and let yourself take you to where you need to go. Can you slowly start to trust your inner Self to know what you need to honor your *True Self*.

Everything that came up is your own inner *Self* talking to you. It may have been a long time since any of your parts got to talk to you or to hear what each other is feeling. It can be a lot to take in and it is important to give yourself time to absorb what you have been holding inside for so long. It is also important to complete the process, and that involves acting on the information that has come up.

Reflection work is very powerful, and it can be liberating to release what may have been buried deep within for quite a long time. However, it is not healthy to reflect without a way to move past it. For example, if your *heart* has told you that it is so very sad and feels so very lonely, then to simply sit and stay in that sadness will not do you, or your heart, any good. What will help is to acknowledge your heart, to let it know you have heard it, and to then take the steps to help it to heal and to become whole again.

This is where the real healing takes place, this is where you begin to really reconnect with yourself and begin to honor yourself. It is in this process that pain, loss, isolation, confusion, separation, regret, anger, bitterness, helplessness and all the other emotions you have felt and suppressed get to have their voice. It is where they get to be listened to and to be heard, and in so doing, get to be released.

Look back at each section and allow yourself to go where each part of you wishes to go in order to heal and grow.

Let the guidance sit with you and hold space with it.

What do you now need to do to bring the needs of your Heart, Mind, Spirit, Soul and Body into your reality? What steps can you follow to be more true to yourself? Take the time to tune in and see what you now need to do to become balanced, healed and whole.

Are your parts in unison? What can you do to give them what they need, what steps do you need to take so that they can shine. How can you honor them and thereby honor yourself. What did your Heart say to you? How does it feel? What do you need to look at and heal? What did your Mind say? What is it needing at this time? What did your Spirit say? What did your Soul say? What did your Body say? What do they need from you to be whole and balanced? What do you need from you?

Take a moment and reflect on each of your parts and what has come up for you - from you.

What I now need to do to honor my True Self...

What I now need to do for my Heart is...

_____
_____
_____
_____
_____

What I now need to do for my Mind is…

_____

_____

_____

_____

_____

What I now need to do for my Spirit is…

_____

_____

_____

_____

_____

What I now need to do for my Soul is…

_____

_____

_____

_____

_____

What I now need to do for my Body is…

_____

_____

_____

_____

_____

This is now your guide, use it and most importantly follow it, it is your compass to yourself!

Learning to let Mind Rest

In order to remain open and receptive to ourselves and all our parts, we need to teach them how to continue to communicate with each other. A lot of the time this means learning to quiet and still the mind so you can hear them easily and with peace.

The mind traditionally is held in esteem for its greatness, and it is great. It is one of the most beautiful and most powerful tools we have at our disposal as human beings. It is strong and mighty and possesses great power and will, and its sheer might is not to be underestimated.

The saying "just put your mind to it" is accurate, because the mind is a logical strategizer. It naturally focuses on what it wants and, despite obstacles, will keep going until it achieves its want, or rationally realizes other avenues to pursue. It does not let go willingly, and will push you even when you don't want to be pushed.

It is constantly trying to figure things out and always looking to find ways to reach its goal. All the while it nudges you on, believing in its own power to reach its destination. The mind is so strong however that most of the time it believes that it is the one in control and that it is its job to solely look after you.

The mind, believing it has your best interests at heart, marches you on, leading you through your life. It decides what you want, what is best for you, how you should handle and approach situations and people in your life. It is cautious and careful and will analyze and assess each step you take, logically putting pieces together and coming up with probable outcomes for you to consider, and this is great.

But the mind in all its glory is not solely responsible for your wellbeing, and it is not, as it would like to believe, capable of solely maintaining your wellbeing. Despite it believing in its own invincibility, it actually needs to work, communicate and know your other essential and beautiful parts; your Heart, your Soul, your Spirit and your Body.

Once you free the mind of its grasp on the responsibility it believes it has, the rest will follow. No one part of you is in control, all of you is, all of you together in harmony and balance, all assisting each other, all knowing each other. Give the mind permission to rest and continue to get to know your other essential beautiful parts so you can discover your spiritual, whole, organic *Self.*

Initiating the steps to Healing and Reactivating Self

Having connected and communicated with your Heart, Mind, Spirit, Soul and Body. You are now ready to begin the process of giving all your parts the space they need to be, so that you can continue to be in harmony with yourself, peacefully and with ease. The following step brings you into a deep a beautiful meditation with your Self, your whole "Self."

Meditation: Reactivating Your Whole Organic Self

Take a few moments and sit quietly stilling your thoughts, breathe slowly and evenly in and out for a count of three. In, 1… 2… 3… Out, 1… 2… 3… do this several times imagining white healing light filling and surrounding you with every breathe; In, 1… 2… 3… Out, 1… 2… 3… In, 1… 2… 3… Out, 1… 2… 3… continue slowly. Then place your hands on your lap with your palms facing upwards, breathe in one deep breath, place your hands over your Heart and imagine going inside yourself and continue breathing normally.

You should be completely relaxed now and in a quite space within yourself. I want you to imagine a white mist surrounding you with a beautiful silver lining, this is your energy shield and it will keep the healing white light in, nourishing you with healing energy and keeping you safe and protected. Take in a long slow centering breath and release it slowly going further into yourself.

Re-activating Self

Now start with your Heart, and ask it to help you to heal it. Then ask your Mind to trust your Heart. Thank it for its help and assistance and allow it to rest a while. Then ask your Spirit to wake up and breathe life energy into your healing process. Tell it you are ready. Feel yourself in your Body and thank it for all it allows you to do, tell it you thank it for everything it does for you, and you are going to look after it as it looks after you. Then if your eyes are open, close them for a moment, relax your Body and take in a long slow deep breath, hold it and release out slowly and steadily. Now smile to yourself and say hello to your Soul, and connect. Ask your Soul to continue to guide you through your life. Tell it you are now open to hearing all it has to teach you.

Now say hello to your Heart, your Mind, your Spirit, your Soul and your Body, tell them that you are sorry for not always listening to them, thank them all and tell them that from now on in you want them all to work, share, know and listen to each other, that they are all important and you need them all equally. Take in one long slow even breath, hold it for three seconds and release it, and open your eyes. You have now started the first step in reactivating your *Whole Self* and initiating the steps in your own healing.

This is now your map to yourself, follow it and see where it brings you. Continue to listen to your own guidance and all of your parts. You have the wisdom of your Soul to follow, enjoy the journey and see where you take yourself. Give thanks and go and get on with your day. Get up and walk it off. Get out into the air even if just for five minutes and breathe in life energy, take the time to look around you at nature, at the sky, the trees, birds or any animals you can see. Breathe in and give thanks for being alive and getting to experience the life you are here to live.

Affirmation: I now accept all the loving gifts of the Universe into my life and I ask for all my parts, Heart, Mind, Spirit, Soul and Body to act in unison with each other and my Higher Self for the betterment of my Highest Good and Greatest Joy. Thank You God - And So It Is.

Journal time...

Take some time and think about an aspect from this chapter that stood out to you or resonated with you and write about it in your journal.

Exercise: Affirmations for You

Take out your journal and write down an affirmation that you will work with for the next seven days. Make it positive and clear, using precise language that describes what you wish to create and nurture in yourself and put it in the present tense.

IAM...

Living our Dreams

Open your Heart and find your Dreams.
Let your Spirit fly as your Soul guides you
to manifest the life you came here to live.

Reconnecting: Me Myself and I

I came and dwelled upon my name, and what was I to see...was all that I had thought I was, was yet to come to be.

Who are you, what is your name, what does it mean, where do you come from, what are your likes, what are your essences, what are the things that give you a sense of happiness, of peace, of adventure? Reconnecting is about exactly that. It is about reconnecting with who you are, the things you like, your essences, and getting to know yourself all over again. It is about getting you to think about yourself and your life and to remind yourself about the things you love to do.

Coming back to My Bliss

What is bliss? What does it feel like? What place does it have in our lives? What awakens your senses, what gives you a feeling of peace, what makes your heart smile? What takes your breath away? What gives you a sense of freedom, what touches your Soul?

Your bliss could be listening to a particular piece of music, it could be taking a scented bubble bath, going for a walk, painting a sunset, watching a sunset, being in nature, being by the sea, singing, dancing, swimming, sitting by an open fire, playing with your children, getting a massage, climbing a mountain, standing on a mountain, laughing with friends, smelling a lily, a rose, hearing a bird tweet, cooking a favorite dish…sharing that dish with those you love, talking with good friends, laughing at a funny movie.

The list of what lightens our hearts and brings joy to us is endless and everyone has their own special things that give them their own sense of bliss. Take a few moments and think about the things that give you a sense of bliss!

When you enrich your own life you enrich the world. By lightening your heart with joy and connecting with the beauty and essence of life you allow yourself to be a vessel of the beauty of all that exists in this world.

Reality Check

Our reality is what we choose to live in, it's the people we choose to associate with, it's where we choose to live, where we work, it's the people and situations we choose to surround ourselves with – its our friends, our lovers, our colleagues, our peers. It's what books we read, our choice of newspapers, what television programs we watch, which news broadcasts, what magazines, what music, our hobbies, sport, music, art, dance.

All these things we choose to be surrounded by and participate and partake in, determine our reality. But it is also how we choose to think. What we believe. What we hold true and untrue. We decide. We determine our reality and we have the power to shape how we want it to be. We create and live in our own reality and this world, this reality, is full of differences, full of complexities, but also full of a simple *Truth*. This truth is our compass in life and our Soul is our guide. Staying on course means using our compass and listening to our Soul. Getting lost simply means we have lost our compass and forgotten how to connect with ourselves.

Getting in touch with the reality you are currently living in helps you to see where you are. Whatever is going on in your life right now is important to notice, as life often has a way of giving us what we need and that might not necessarily be what we want. So look deeply and see if there is an element of you that is being encouraged to awaken and strengthen. Take a few minutes and think about how your life is right now at this moment in time, at this moment in your journey. Are you on your right path? Are you being honest with your Self and with your own truth? Are you living your dream?

Uncovering our Dreams

Uncovering and allowing our dreams to exist is sometimes difficult to do, because our dreams are what we hold deep in our heart and it takes great courage to live in our hearts. It is our hearts that are our *True Selves,* and it is only by learning to live in our hearts that we can uncover the truth of our Soul and discover our dreams.

Sometimes our thoughts act to form barriers to our heart, and over our lives we unconsciously, in times of hurt or confusion, block our Spirit from forming its mission and fulfilling its destiny. Knowing that you recognize your heart lifts your Spirit and illuminates it. Connecting with it brings a force of life energy into your being that will carry you through your life with purpose, peace and joy. Following our dreams means being true to ourselves in our hearts, and learning to trust in the process of life, and in our capability as creative beings to manifest our own reality and live our life in truth and beauty, which is the essence of who we are.

The Path to Manifesting our Dreams

Everyone has dreams and aspirations that they hold deep within. Sometimes these dreams find it hard to manifest into our reality because we have developed thoughts around what we think they should be or could be, and not what we dream them to be.

Allowing our dreams to manifest requires us to look honestly at our own areas of self-worth, self-esteem, confidence, values and beliefs, and further to see what limiting thought forms we are holding in our subconscious that may be blocking us from fulfilling them. Clearing negative or restrictive thought patterns and past pain allows us to go forward. Learning to unblock your blocks will allow you to tap into your dreams and give them the room they need to be.

Living our dreams means allowing ourselves to be open to what they might be. This requires us to allow our dreams to *dream*, and further to use our creativity to help them come into our existence. Discovering and shaping our dreams into reality means not just working with our Minds, but also with our Hearts, our Spirit our Soul and our Body.

Bringing your *Dreams* and your *Self* into alignment means creating the *IS* you truly want to see in your life. Before you delve into your Dreams, learn to clear your mind of limitation, both your own and that which you have learned and taken on from others, and free your Self of any negative past attachments and what you may have believed was real for you. The truth is, we create our own reality by how and what we believe. When we believe in limitation, we experience limitation. When we believe in pain, we experience pain. When we believe in our own suffering we experience suffering.

Finding these thoughts in ourselves and releasing them allows us to be free in mind and further allows the mind to work at manifesting the destiny of your Soul. When we believe in ourselves and follow our hearts we experience a world full of possibility. When we trust our Spirit we experience a world full of choices, and our dreams and reality become mirrors of our Soul.

Exercise: Reality Check-in

Get your journal out and without thinking too hard answer question 1 below. Don't analyze, just write it as it is, e.g. I am… I live… I work… etc. etc. Then read over what you wrote and see what you think about it. Really think about it. Then follow on and answer question 2. You can do this exercise as often as you like. It allows you to check in with your reality and see how close you are to the reality you would like to be experiencing.

Question 1: What is My Reality?

_____

_____

_____

_____

_____

_____

Question 2: What is the reality I would like to see in my life?

_____

_____

_____

_____

_____

_____

Taking the Lead in Your Life

In order to take the lead in your life you need to know where you want to go, and you also need to learn to be able to see how you can change your _IS_ to reflect your new chosen reality.

This means learning to notice and eliminate hidden negative thought forms that you have learned to believe in about yourself and the world you live in. Once you do this you can then turn them into positive loving manifestations and bring them forward into your Now.

Learn to catch your thoughts, and look at them, then question why you had that thought and see where it really came from. Is it attached to an old memory or a painful past experience? Is it still true for you? Are you able to let it go? If you don't like the thought, change it.

If it's not a positive or constructive thought, change it. If you do not believe you can, then journal about it and ask yourself why you are holding onto it. Is there a genuine fear attached to it? Do you need to do some healing around it? Delve into it and bring out the truth about it. Then heal it. Be in the truth of your thoughts and make them work for you. Be your own master of your own mind and listen to yourself as you move yourself forward in your life.

You are Your World - Learning to break out of illusions

It's a simple psychology with tremendous effect. Imagine a ripple in the ocean caused by a small pebble being thrown in. It makes a small impact and ripples out creating an outward replica of itself. It pulses out and out until it joins again with the ocean. This is how our mind works.

We hold thoughts, and they replicate and become our experiences. Over the course of our lives we develop ways of thinking about ourselves and of our world based on our life experiences and on our conditioning. We often forget that we have the power to shape our thoughts, and that taking responsibility for them is up to us. Think positive thoughts and you will have positive experiences, think negative thoughts and you will have negative experiences, and know while you're thinking that you have the power to choose and change the thoughts you make.

Everyone has some form of conditioning that they have learned to believe in be it from society or family or past relationships. Taking responsibility for your *Self* and your *Life* is about taking responsibility for your choices of thought, and learning to un-condition yourself, so that you can decide on the types of thoughts you will hold in your psyche. Do this by learning to see where you may be blocking yourself. Then allow yourself to be open and honest and unblock yourself and begin living your NOW your WAY. Making YOUR journey not from a place of fear, negativity and limits, but from a place of awareness, space and expansion, where you lead yourself through the myriad of possibilities that are open to you. Do so knowing that you have the capacity and power necessary for fulfilling your life. A life bathed in peace, joy, understanding, love, happiness and harmony.

Getting to know Yourself – Thoughts and all

The process of unraveling thought forms takes time. It is not a quick fix. It is a process, a process that you can learn to incorporate into your everyday life until it becomes both natural and instinctual. It is the process of getting to know yourself and how your mind has learned to adjust to your subjective surroundings.

From a very early age we are open to assimilation from those around us. We take on cultural, societal, religious, racial, economic and even family beliefs that have been handed down generation after generation. And then we go and say things such as, "It's not my fault, its just the way I am. I can't help it! It's who I am... I've always been like this." Really? Have you? Or have you learned to be like that? Have you learned to think the way you think? Really think about it. Where did you get the thoughts you have? Where did you learn to believe in the things you do? Where did you learn to believe you are the way you are, or your life is the way it is?

We so often in life learn to see ourselves through the eyes and opinions of others that we forget to believe in our own greatness. Years of conditioning, by and to one another, lead us to denying ourselves the freedom to express our *True Selves*, and further lead to us believing in the limits we are told exist. This is shifting more now, as more and more people are stepping out of the shadows and proclaiming themselves as who they really are, the way being paved for the rest of us to follow.

Change your IS - Change your Thoughts

Responsibility for your thoughts lies with you. The power of control over your thoughts lies with you. You, and you alone have the power to determine the quality of life and experiences you will have. The first relationship you have in this life is with yourself. You do not have power over any other being and they do not have power over you. If you think otherwise you are simply wasting your time and energy, and focusing your own issues outside of yourself.

The way your life is now, is the way it is. There is no fault. There just is. If you are not happy with your life then change your *is*, and stop running around in fault or restriction, including your own. Creating blame is an escape for not taking action. Waiting for the world to come along and help you out is living in an illusion, and places you in a state of victimhood. You are your world and it is you who helps you. You are the only one in a position of power over your life. Begin there and take action and responsibility for your Self and for your life. That is what you came here to do.

Mind Your Mind - Attracting in the Positive

Remember your power and stay aware. Limiting thoughts have a way o f keeping us locked down into believing untruths about ourselves, our abilities and our personal power. Whenever you find yourself believing in a thought of separation or limitation, actively set about changing it by turning it around and making a positive affirmation out of it.

First write down the negative thought, let it be heard, acknowledge it and find its source. Then switch it to the positive and write it down on a piece of paper and carry it around with you. Read it several times a day silently and out loud building up your personal power. It may take a week, a month, a year to become real for you, but just keep at it until you finally know you believe what you are saying and you feel the shift deep inside.

Both positive and negative thoughts have the power to manifest, so be mindful of what you put out into the universe for manifestation. Believe something long enough and strong enough and it will manifest. Both positive and negative thoughts have the energy to exist, so choose carefully what you think. Remember, you are the creator of your world and you alone have the power to create a life you love. Believe in your ability and believe in your dreams, then start creating them, one step at a time.

Exercise: My Five Great Wants

Start by doing a bit of background research with yourself. Think of some instances in your life when there has been something you have really wanted or currently really want in your life. It could be a want to be the best footballer, athlete, swimmer, ballerina, singer, actor, writer, artist... or it could be that you want to take an adventure holiday around the world, visit Africa, Alaska, Hawaii...spend a summer drinking wine and eating olives, or a year out teaching computer skills to farmers in West Africa.

You might really want to settle down, get married, have children, retire, write your memoirs, take dance classes, learn a musical instrument, do volunteer work. Or there could be a dream job you would just love to have. Maybe you have wanted to chuck it all in and go back to further your education, learn to paint, become a photographer, teach yoga, design web sites, learn to fly, become a community development worker, a life coach, a musician, a vet, a nurse, learn about the environment, grow your own vegetables, move to the country, move country, dance, swim, sing!

The possibilities are endless, so try not to limit yourself. Just be fun and free with letting your wants out. So what are your wants? Make a list of them below or in your journal and then look at them and pick out your top 5.

My Wants in Life and Love...

_____

_____

_____

_____

_____

_____

_____

_____

_____

_____

Next Step: Unblocking Blocks - Finding the Hidden Fears in My Thoughts

Now pick out a **Want** and write down the feelings and thoughts you hold about it. Start with your first thoughts and follow their natural sequence as they enter into your mind. Really imagine that you are on the cusp of going to go and do your **Want,** or are just about to start making plans to bring it into existence. What do you think about yourself doing this?

Be deeply honest with yourself and really push yourself at imagining it as you really feel it. If you find your thoughts leading you to make excuses for not doing your want, or you find yourself not believing in your capabilities to do it, just note them, and write them down. Ask yourself how you really feel about doing it and actually making it happen for real, for yourself.

What I really feel and think about it...

_____

_____

_____

_____

_____

_____

If you find you have some hidden blocks, respect them by acknowledging them.

Start by writing out the fears that you have about achieving it...

_____

_____

_____

_____

_____

_____

Ask your fear what it is doing for you. Is it helping you or hindering you? If it is helping you then sit into it and ask it to guide you to make healing, positive, enriching changes that assist you to grow and build the life you dream of. If its hindering you then release it and let it go.

Complete the cycle now with a personal affirmation stating your worth, value and belief in your want.

Make a positive Affirmation for yourself...

_____
_____
_____
_____
_____

Affirmations:
I use my mind for creative expression.
I believe in the endless possibilities that are open to me.
I hold only positive loving thoughts for manifestation in my life.

The mind is a part of evolution just like you, nature, and the world. Thoughts naturally then fit in with this cycle. They too evolve, flow, grow, change, renew and expand. Allowing the flow towards evolution allows it to its proper place, expansion. Keeping it small, locked, blocked or in any other limiting manner – stops, falters and hinders your own growth and that of human kind and the natural universal flow of life.

Moving into the Creative Realm

Having completed the steps in uncovering limiting thought patterns in relation to your wants and desires, you have also learned how to recognize in yourself when you are having limiting thoughts and further how to put them aside and live in positive possibility-driven thoughts.

Our subconscious mind has will and power, and if you believe in yourself, then your dream will believe in you too, because it is a manifestation of you. Following it is knowing it, and becoming it is being it. Begin simply by getting in touch with what it is you dream and leave all thoughts of limitation and negativity out. Only allow thoughts that are positive to exist.

Exercise: The Dream Bubble – Allowing Creativity In

Draw a large circle and write your name underneath it. Now look at the blank circle and imagine your dream is inside it. This circle is blank, nothing exists in it except what you choose to put in it.

Take a couple of minutes and stare into the circle allowing your *Mind* to comprehend the endless possibilities that could come to fill that circle. Think about all the things you want to do in your life no matter how bizarre or simple they seem to you.

Think deeply and connect with your True Self

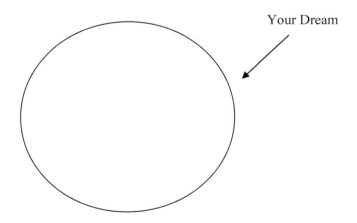

Affirmation: I now manifest my deepest Self into my Heart and into my Life.

Now bring in your Heart, ask it what it truly desires. Keep staring into your dream circle filling it with the energy of your Heart. Then bring in your Soul, ask it to help show you your life path. Pause and breathe deeply, then bring in your Spirit and ask it to guide you towards realizing your dream. Keep looking into the blank circle and dream. Dream long and dream slow. Go in and in, letting your *Soul Self* take you to it.

Imagining Your Dream into Reality

Then when you get it bring the dream forward into your consciousness from your Heart and quite simply start imagining it into your reality. It is here in the realm of fantasy that the imagination can tap into its creativity and feed your dream back to you. When you feel you know deep in your Heart what it is you Dream of, write it down, and as it manifests in ink on the page in front of you, imagine it manifest with the same ease into your life.

Manifesting My Dream: Think - Feel - Imagine - Be

Write down how you would like your dream to be and keep it in the present tense, as if you are living it right now.

In my dream I am...

_____
_____
_____
_____
_____
_____
_____
_____
_____
_____
_____

This is your dream, keep it safe and nurture it.
Let it take roots and begin to grow.

Journal Time...

Take some time and think about an aspect from this chapter that stood out to you or resonated with you and write about it in your journal.

Exercise: Make It So

In your journal dedicate a page to your dream. You can make a collage of pictures that inspire you or even draw a picture of it. Write down key words that represent it to you and if it helps make out a list of things you need to learn or do to help bring it into reality.

Exercise: Vision Board

Take it a step further and make a vision board of your dream. Be creative and have fun with it. Cut out pictures from magazines or print out or draw images that reflect it clearly. Then stick it up on your wall and every day let your dream be fed back into you so that it grows and takes shape in your conscious mind.

Part Two

Healing in Heart

Life is a journey in understanding
who we truly are, and coming back into our hearts.

Love – Opportunity for growth

Life's journey is always about leading us back to love. How that path manifests for us in our chosen life journey can be very different for each of us as individuals. But as Spirits living a human existence we all have a connection of heart and we all feel the same pain, it is just our stories that may differ. We are brought together to love because we are meant to be on particular journeys with one another. We all have life lessons to learn and teach each other, and we are here to connect and bring each other back into our hearts. Love of all kinds is precious, it is the breath of life that we all require, to be who we aspire to be.

Falling In Love

Falling in love is one of the most transformative and significant experiences our hearts encounter. It often acts as a catalyst for change that we seek but are not always aware we need. It brings us into and out of ourselves; it pushes us to face issues about ourselves and our emotions and to come face to face with who we really are.

It is a time when we enter into the realms of bliss, self-doubt, confusion, adventure and great joy, and if we can take a leap in Soul, it offers a connection of Heart that can transcend our very being.

Love in its essence is a transformational experience. It is a meeting of divine union where Souls unite and offer a sacred space in which to share the development of heart. Taking a journey of *Heart* with another human being is a sacred act, that once taken acts to cast out hidden embers of the flame of our true selves, pushing us to move more and more firmly into our consciousness and into our deepest being.

Learning in Relationships

We learn in life through all our relationships. As children, we begin with our family and the caregivers in our lives, then through our friendships, and then through romantic encounters. If we are lucky, it starts all over again when we too have the privilege to raise children and we get to experience the unique love a person encounters when they are the caregivers, the nurturers, the life protectors and they get to understand the deep bond of raising a child and what it means to love unconditionally.

This cycle continues all throughout life. All our relationships are different, and we get something out of every single encounter we have. Certain relationships will teach us more than others. It all depends on what we are seeking in ourselves in that time. We are drawn naturally to people depending on our essence, our energy and our capacity to connect with them. Certain people attract to one another and bring out a side that can remain hidden with others and within one's *Self.*

In all our interaction there is a place for growth and healing, and a space in which you can gain a better understanding of your *Self* and your *Soul,* and live more and more in your heart. All relationships teach if we are willing to see the lessons and take them on board. Look and see who is in your life right now and see what reflection you see in them. See what you may be seeking at this time, and what you can learn from them. Healing relationships along the journey of life enables us to grow and expand in awareness, and as we shift up, we continue to heal the relationships that came before. As we grow and develop, we begin to heal the splits that occurred as children. We keep moving up and in, and as we do, we continue to learn, we continue to grow, and we continue to embody our highest, most conscious *Self*.

Looking at and reflecting on key relationships in your life will help you see where your place of healing began, and further to see the lessons and journey you placed yourself in as a Soul. Do so, in love and understanding, and keep yourself centered in your own grace.

Hearts Break

Hearts break, it's a fact. Some crack a bit, some splinter, some split right in two. Sometimes the heartbreak is so strongly felt we can find ourselves left with big holes that we don't know how to fill. We find ourselves left with questions and doubts, insecurities, hurt, blame and sadness. Sometimes we are filled with a loss that if we let it, will consume us and pull us in so that we lose our very Souls in it.

Yet these emotions and confusions are often what we need to help us to build ourselves back up. These heartbreaks are necessary for us to experience, to understand, to feel our capacity to be human. These heartbreaks teach us how to love and why to love. We need them, and we need to go through them. Even the darkest ones teach, for they reach our Soul and they silence us so that we can connect, so that we can feel, so that we can see our capacity of Spirit, of Soul, of Mind and of Heart, in ourselves and in everyone around us. We may not think it at the time, but broken hearts heal just as much as they break.

The Heart and Mind Give Up

There may come a point in your life where you truly wonder how much pain a heart can take, that surely it will just stop, that it isn't possible to hold so much pain, that it is shattered in so many pieces it can never be put back together. There may come a point when the mind starts to lose faith, as the pain of the heart troubles the mind. It constantly asks it for help, to understand what has happened and why it has happened. The mind struggles with these constant questions that it cannot answer. And the mind being the mind does not want to give up because he is the mind, he is leader. Over time the mind builds with frustration and gets angry with the heart as it cannot answer its questions about love and pain.

And so the heart, deeply hurt and alone, gives up. It decides not to love again and to stop trying to figure it all out. The mind, too, gives up and decides to not waste any more of its time with the heart's constant questions, for it tells itself the heart is foolish and can deal with its own problems. Enough of its time has been wasted with silly questions about love and pain. And so, the two stop talking.

The heart buries itself deep inside, hoping that it will be forgotten about. The mind, too, decides to forget about the heart and distracts itself with new challenges and tasks. And so, the upset heart and the upset mind upset the Soul, for the Soul can see their pain and wants to help them, but they have cut themselves off from each other, believing they can make it on their own.

Oh, *L'amour*

So what do we do when love comes back to us and hits us with its magic spell? What can we do when we find we cannot resist its magnetic pull? We may try to resist, but love's power is not to be denied and its sweet scent will follow us and intoxicate us with its power to transform our reality and slip us under its spell. Sometimes its power is so overwhelming it takes us over and we begin to feel we are no longer the ones in control of our lives.

It is like a force outside of ourselves is calling the shots. We battle with our hearts and our minds and we try to maintain our control but somehow we find our happiness begins to be measured by our ability to maintain a harmonious relationship with the one who has, as we so often put it, stolen our heart.

The Magic of Love

When love comes knocking at our door it's nearly impossible to send it away, because love is who we are, and it is in this shared experiencing of love that we shine as human beings. It cannot be denied, because to deny love is to deny oneself. And so, somewhat cautiously, we learn to let ourselves open up once more, and we allow ourselves to love again.

Before we know it, we're stepping out of our safety cocoon and back into an oasis of passion, joy, exhilaration, vulnerability, happiness, and sheer and wonderful bliss. It's the yin and yang of it all that makes it so darn exciting, and so we go from closed and safe to curious and open, and it all happens in 0.5 seconds. Before we know it we are back in the love circle and adventure and connection is looming around the corner, waiting for a way in.

Not all love relationships are meant to be forever, some are chapters in our story and are there to help us to grow and develop. This can be hard to accept, especially when it has been a deep and profound connection. What happens when this love, this magic, this joy begins to look like it will leave as quickly as it came, and we find ourselves fearful of a life without. Back to just us, alone and sad, and all the more confused for having experienced love. What do we do, what can we do? Do we vow never to fall in love again, do we pray for salvation, do we cry, do we close up our hearts?

Or do we heal, learn from the connection we experienced, and move on knowing that the circle of love will come back to us. Because when it comes to *l'amour* we know all too well that we will be unable to stop its magic force from entering our hearts, because it is magic, and it is beautiful, and it has a power all of its own.

So we take our past pain and we move ourselves forward, hoping that this time love will stay, that this time love will win, that this time love will not leave. That by now we have learned how to be in relationship, learned how to be honest, learned how to nurture it, honor it, and our own *Self*-worth is strong enough not to be fooled by false declarations. We now know that love is what you do, not just what you say. By now we are healthy, we are happy in our own Selves, and we are whole in our own capacity as human beings, wiser for the life experiences we have had. Now it is time to share this journey. Now it is time to shine.

If you feel you can't face losing the connection of love, reach inside your *Heart* and love yourself, because the only love the heart can't bear to lose is yours. This love will keep you warm; it will give you strength and keep you sweet. It will also act to attract a mirror love in someone who matches your vibration. Love yourself and the love in your heart will attract a love of pure intention in another, and the two loves will rejoice in finding each other.

Yes, the steps to get to here can be paved with pain and much confusion but they can also be filled with much joy, love, insight and so much happiness.

The Soul loves to grow, and each inch of growth makes your Soul dance and sing with delight and it gives the heart hope and enthusiasm to continue on. It lifts you up, so you can go on continuing your journey with hope and faith, for your Soul is happy, joyous and delighted when you are listening to it. It will not lead you astray. It is bringing you to where your Soul wanted to go so that you can learn to love yourself from the heart of your Soul, not the ego, and in doing so find a love of truth with another. Thank it and bless yourself and others and simply let love live.

Breaking Through Illusions of Conduct

Illusions of conduct, behavior and reality continue because people participate in their untruth, be it their own or someone else's. And it is this continuance that brings and carries blockages with us everywhere we go. Self love is the liberator that allows you to see the Truth and further to reclaim your own *True Self*. If, by any chance, the person you are with is pushing you down or hindering your growth, then you must look after you. The only alternative is to stay and be knocked down, pushed back or sat on top of, and that is not really an alternative.

Healing your *Self* and giving yourself love is what ultimately allows you to become whole and further helps you to cut through any illusions you may be holding about love and self-worth and your issues with it. When we are able to truly love ourselves from our Soul and not our ego, then we can truly love others, and our relationships will begin to mirror this love and manifest what is inside our heart, our core, out into our lives.

Show yourself love unconditionally, and keep doing so, over and over again. You are your Heart, it is your truest form and it is your responsibility to nurture your heart with love, care and compassion for yourself. The buck stops with you, so love yourself and love your *Heart* and allow it to blossom and grow.

It is ok to love.
It is ok to want to be loved.
That is what we came here to do.

Exercise: Taking the Steps to Emotional Healing

Find yourself a quiet place, and what I mean by quiet is go somewhere where no one you know is going to interrupt you in your thoughts. Take yourself to a nice café, go on a train ride, or lie in bed and stare at the ceiling - whatever you do just be alone, and be with yourself.

This exercise can be used to find insights to many situations you have had, or are having in your life, and it will help you find your true answers to matters of inner confusion or illusion whether you are currently aware of them or not.

Before you start, take some time and think about a person that you have had a connection of heart with. It may be romantic, or it may be a part of your childhood, be it neglect, abandonment or feeling unloved or unwanted. When you have chosen something take a few moments here to connect with whatever comes to mind. Allow yourself to hold yourself in a safe and loving space and give your heart and your mind permission to allow all that has been held within to come out of you for healing. Then begin the process of complete and total, honest reflection.

Why do I feel the way I do?
What are these emotions?
Why do I have them?
Where did they come from?

Every time you get to an answer, ask; *is this the soul truth or ego truth?* Only stop asking when you get the *Soul-Truth* answer. This can be uncomfortable for the ego, so know that and carry through untill you know deep inside that you are answering from your deepest center, the center that has no judgement, no punishment, only compassion, understanding and love. Learn from your answers and grow from them.

Part One: How I feel - It is important when doing the first part of this exercise to allow yourself to move through each step of your emotions and allow yourself to feel them just as you did in the past, right up to how you do now. Don't overthink it and don't analyze it, just feel it. You will know immediately if what you are feeling is real or not. Your heart does not lie, and it does not judge, so allow absolutely no room for any judgement of any kind to exist in any part of you. Just go through it, feel it and be honest with yourself. There is no one here you are trying to kid.

This is just you with you, and it is a growing and understanding experience, so experience it and allow yourself to grow in it. It is all held inside you. Now it is time to let it go. So, close your eyes for a moment and connect with your *Heart.* Then write down how you feel, be honest with yourself and love yourself as if you are a child who needs protection. Let yourself experience how you felt with your heart, go through the feelings of the past and allow it all to come out on the page. Write down everything that you recall and don't let your mind interrupt you. If it does, just ask it to be quiet and to wait, it will have its turn. Keep going until you are finished. When the pen stops, don't read what you wrote. Just smile and give thanks for allowing it to come out. Use the space provided or if you require more room, please use your journal.

And so begin...

How I feel...

_____
_____
_____
_____
_____
_____
_____
_____
_____
_____
_____
_____
_____
_____
_____
_____
_____

Charity Amy Murphy

Part Two: What I think - Settle into yourself and this time engage with your *Mind*. Ask yourself questions and allow yourself to go back again and write what you think about it all. What do you think of this time in your life now? What did you think of it then? Where were you in yourself at the time? What was or is your relationship with this person? Ask questions that help you uncover your hidden thoughts that are still lingering within you. Keep going and ask and answer as many questions that come up for you until you have nothing left to ask and the pen in your hand stops writing.

What I think…

_____

_____

_____

_____

_____

_____

_____

_____

_____

_____

_____

_____

_____

_____

_____

_____

_____

_____

_____

_____

Charity Amy Murphy

When you are finished writing take a minute to clear your mind, and then read what you have written right from the start of this session beginning with; *How I feel* - up to *What I think*. Remember there is no blame or judgment here, only awareness, growth and love. This is a very powerful exercise and it can bring up a lot, so be gentle with yourself and hold yourself in divine peace and love.

Part Three: Insights to Myself - Now at the top of a new page write: "*Reading back on what I have written I have learned a lot about myself and what I have been holding deep within me. I see now that …*" and continue writing until the pen in your hand stops and there is nothing left for you to say at this moment.

Reading back through what I have written, I now see…

_____

_____

_____

_____

_____

_____

_____

_____

_____

_____

_____

_____

_____

_____

_____

_____

_____

_____

_____

Charity Amy Murphy

When you are finished sit quietly, close your eyes and breathe in deeply for the count of five, hold for ten seconds and exhale for the count of five... and imagine that with each *in-breath* you are clearing yourself of all thoughts and feelings, and with each *out-breath* you are releasing all that came up. Repeat this three times in total, now ... Breathe In... 1,2,3,4,5 Hold... 1,2,3,4,5,6,7,8,9,10 Breathe Out... 1,2,3,4,5 Breathe In... 1,2,3,4,5 Hold... 1,2,3,4,5,6,7,8,9,10 Out... 1,2,3,4,5 In... 1,2,3,4,5 Hold... 1,2,3,4,5,6,7,8,9,10 Out... 1,2,3,4,5...continue breathing softly and let all tension leave your body.

Feel good in yourself for allowing yourself to be open and honest with yourself and for taking the courage to go back and really see yourself in your relationships of heart and mind. Release all, and then go and drink a glass of water, stretch out your legs and give thanks for the healing and awakening process you just went through.

Learn, Love, and Live. This is your purpose. By accepting, you are loving, by realizing, you are bringing it into your *Heart*, you are transforming it into love.

We are all loved all the time. All the time.

Answers for My Healing Heart

Trusting in love means trusting in people and knowing that everybody seeks and wants to be loved and to love. It also means that we must learn to love ourselves, for only then can we learn to be loved by others as we truly desire. The final step in this sequence involves the releasing of all that has been held so far, deep inside your heart for clearing and setting free. In order to do this you need to ask yourself honestly; *Am I willing now to see, and to let go of past – to move to future? Am I ready to jump - or am I still in fear. Still in blame. Still in ego. Still in pain.*

If you are ready, then repeat the following and move on.

"I now release, and I let go, all that I am
holding in my Heart for healing.

I now heal my Heart releasing, the past
with love, the past with light.

I Am free of all that has been.
I Am free of all that I've seen.
I Am free to carry on.
I Am free to truly belong.

I release and I let go.
I begin to heal and know.
I move forward.
And I move on.

I now sing my sweetest song."

Connect with your *Heart* and say to yourself

"I AM my Heart, I AM my True Heart, I AM my Highest Vibration"

Then give yourself the answers you need to complete
your healing of heart and write them all down.

Have your pen and journal beside you and let your heart heal.

Answers for my Healing Heart: *This is what I have still been
holding in my heart for healing...this is what I am now setting free.*

I AM My Heart and I release and I let go, all I've been and all I know...

_____

_____

_____

_____

_____

_____

_____

_____

_____

_____

_____

_____

_____

_____

_____

_____

_____

_____

_____

_____

_____

_____

_____

_____

_____

_____

_____

Charity Amy Murphy

_____
_____
_____
_____
_____
_____
_____
_____
_____
_____
_____
_____
_____
_____
_____
_____
_____
_____
_____
_____
_____
_____

*If you need extra space please continue on a
separate sheet or within your journal.*

When you are finished – Close your eyes and allow the
healing vibration of unconditional love expand out and
soothe, comfort and heal you – then repeat again.

"I AM my Heart, I AM my Heart, I AM my True Heart"

Then see, accept, release, heal, forgive and
set it free - it is over - it is gone.
It is past and you are free.

Heal all Relationships

Go back over your life and heal all aspects of past relationships that need healing. Clear all pain and all separation and see the light that has existed along your journey with others, even if that light was your own inner star learning to come forward. In healing all relationships you are healing the separateness that is within yourself and within your *Truth*.

In healing all relationships you are allowing *Truth* to enter and permeate your existence. You are setting yourself free from past emotional ties. You are connecting with your own Soul's love and you are surrendering to the knowledge that love is all there really is. Everything else is an illusion of the ego, an illusion you no longer participate or partake in.

You are stepping above and beyond the pain, and reclaiming your own true nature, your own true heart, your very essence of who you really are. A Soul of grace and love, conscious of your inner light, alert and awake in the world. Gracious and strong in the development of your character, and wise in understanding the *true* from the *untrue*.

Love everyone and everything from your Soul, because everyone and everything in your experience and sense of existence is a part of your story of life and therefore a part of you. By bringing healing to your life and your life stories you are bringing healing to yourself and therefore to the world. You are moving yourself and the world from *wounded* to *healed*, and taking your place in the plan for all humanity. A return to wholeness, a return to peace, a return to *Truth*, a return to Love.

To Love – is to let love live, in our *Hearts* and in our *Souls*. In our days and in our nights. In our interactions with each other and with our world. To Love - is to free love and not be afraid to love. To believe in love, to breathe love. To know it is where we come from, it is where we are going, it is who we are. It is our connection to ourselves and to each other and it is ours to share and to give to each other freely.

So are you ready to jump, or are you still in fear? Your *Soul* knows to go forward - it knows this completely. Your mind may still be working through, trying to make sense of all that has been. It is a process, and one that you need to go through when the time is right for you. Know that when you do, you will realize that everything that you thought you couldn't face will fade and you will see your journey with new eyes and new hope.

Let your heart heal and your mind will catch up. Learn your lessons. Let them soak into your being and allow your *Heart* to open once more. A new way is waiting for you and you are waiting to go forth into your **now.** Once you have done this, you are then able to act as an Earth guide to other *Souls* who have also come to learn and share in this great life experience.

Going through pain and separation yourself you will have learned how to heal, and therefore you can help others to heal, because you have become what is known as a *wounded healer.* Your healing becomes the platform in which you can inspire and help others to heal. Your journey becomes a part of human consciousness, and your shifting and healing of relationships helps to heal the splits in others and acts as a beacon for others to follow. Listen to your heart, it will lead you to your dreams. Follow it to find peace and happiness. Free your mind and the rest will follow. Life is a journey in understanding Love. For when we understand that, we understand ourselves and who we really are. Open your *Heart* and listen to your *Soul* as you guide yourself through your life.

Affirmation:
I now open my Heart to the Truth of all mankind. I now live truely in my Heart for this is the essence of who I AM.

Meditation - The Love Bubble

Close your eyes and clear your mind. Sit in yourself and take some relaxing breaths in and out, in and out, feeling all tension leave your body. Now go inside yourself and feel your Heart. Feel, be, sit with it, hear it, and know what it is that your Heart wants.

Now give your Heart the Love it needs. Sit with it and love it, love all of you and allow it to be.

The Love Bubble

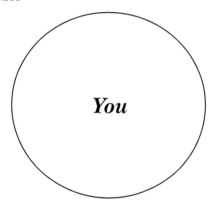

Imagine that an invisible bubble surrounds you. Feel and sense this bubble around you. Then in your mind's eye see that a mist of Love is all around you and pull this mist of Love into your bubble. Bring it in, bring it in, bring it in, and fill your bubble with love. In and in, until you sense the love is in, and your bubble is full of this love. This is your Love bubble and you sit in it always. Allow this mist of **love** soak into your entire being, soothing your entire Soul. See your Heart radiate out the love inside, as all the pain it was holding is dissolved and transformed into pure white light. See your Heart shine with a bright healing light and let it shine out of you, spreading in all directions...

Now give your Heart the love it craves. Sit with it and love it, love all of you. Open yourself up and let yourself feel love, let yourself give love and let yourself receive love. The more love, the more love, on and on it goes. On and on and in and in, just love, and love will keep on loving. Giving love to your *heart* is giving life to your *Soul*. It is giving air to your *body* and wings to your *Spirit*, so that you can soar above the mountain tops and glide through the crisp, cool air, it allows you to shine brightly like the stars in a clear night sky. Give yourself love and surround yourself with love. Follow your heart, it will show you where to go. Relax knowing that you are in the flow of love. Your heart is the gateway to your Soul. Heal your heart. Free your Spirit and follow your path to your Dreams.

Everywhere you now go your bubble of love goes with you. Everyone you meet, your bubble touches with theirs. They meet, they join and love joins - love spreads. It heals and it connects and reawakens the love held within us all.

*Affirmation: Love is in Me and all around,
I AM Love and Love is Me.*

Journal time…

Take some time and think about an aspect from this chapter that stood out to you or resonated with you and write about it in your journal.

Exercise: Those I love

Take some time and write in your journal about those you love and the joy this love brings to your heart.

We are Energy - We are Light

We are energy, we are light.
We are Spirit suspended in form.
Healing comes from within and from
connecting with our light and our Source.

Preparing for Our Soul Journey

Before we come into the world, our *Soul* works with its spiritual guides and picks a life, certain scenarios, experiences and events that will help its *Soul* to grow and learn from. It does this by choosing, experiences, lessons, personality, family, lovers, friends, nationality and sex, then when all the ingredients are ready we pop down into the world of Earth and begin living out our creation.

Some *Souls* enter choosing to take on and learn particular lessons. Some enter choosing to help shift the consciousness of the bloodline they are entering into, and some enter choosing to participate in the divine plan of *Soul Consciousness*. We always have a choice in this life to live it in the light or the dark. To be a vessel of grace or walk in the shadow of the ego. Each of us can seek our own redemption and move away from the dark into the light, this is the gift of free will.

Being Born into Life

It starts here in the realm of the heavens, a bright spark of light shining down from the universe. A Soul waits to be incarnated into the world of life and it waits until the people who are to be its perspective parents on Earth are ready (consciously or unconsciously) in their Soul journey to welcome them into the world.

We grow in the womb of woman, an incubation of energy creating a space, transferring the structures of the human form. One feeding and nourishing the other. That is how bonds and attachments are formed. Our energy builds and develops, as molecules become structures that are built around a vision of life. Our physical body manifests and we download our human existence. That is how we pass down the genetic line absorbing the energy of those that came before us.

When a man and a woman come together to mate, they are not just continuing in the evolution of the human body, but also in the evolution of *Souls* as *Spirit* transferred into human form. The *spiritual energy* of the Soul, on entering the womb, consciously chooses to take on all that the perspective parents have to offer, and energy from both parents mix and match perfectly to that of the *Soul* that is coming into the world.

It is the gift of woman to house another *Spirit* within her being, and there is a very strong importance of, and by, parents in clearing past and present negative attachments, because by coming together to form and make new life, they are transferring what they are carrying energetically down their own genetic line. Both parents need to be consciously open to what they may be transferring, and each need to take responsibility in helping move their respective bloodlines forward for healing.

The Spiritualization of Sex

When we come together with another human being and partake in the spiritual experience of sex, we are moving in and between altering states of consciousness, and we are connecting not only with our own *Soul,* but that of the other person. The exchange of energy within and between electrifies and intensifies as pulsating energy beams pass up and down our spiritual centers, connecting us in the deepest of ways.

It is the gift of sex to experience a spiritual connection of *Soul* and Source. To connect with another human being in this way moves us out of the mind and back out into the consciousness of the Universe. Entwined in *Body* and *Soul* we open up a space and connect with our Spiritual *Self*, here we are free to exist in the realms of existence itself.

In love making we are both grounded by the energy of our Root chakra and transcended through our Crown chakra, as we experience connection and belonging by joining in a union of energy and source. Sex is not just about physical connection, it is also about opening up a space for divine union and a channel for creation itself to move through us. By experiencing the union of sex, we open a channel for the possibility of new life, and in so doing we become vessels in which new life can take form and we, quite literally, can become creators in the world of life. And as we continue our journey in life we continue in the spiritual evolution of *Souls* on *Earth*.

The Chakra System of Consciousness

As Spiritual beings and beings of light we have within our human body wheels of light and energy that are called chakra. These chakra are vortexes and levels of consciousness that fuel our *Spiritual and Physical Body* while we are here on Earth. They are channels of communication between source and form, and they hold within them energetic frequencies that help to harmonize our Soul-body. When they are open, flowing and connected we experience balance, strength and awareness on all levels of our being.

When we are born we are fresh with life force energy. As we make our way through our journey of life we begin to notice how certain things in life can boost and give us energy, and how certain things can diminish it and block it. We begin to understand that when we are free and flowing our energy is free and flowing, and that when we are struggling with something or going against our True or Higher Self our energy becomes stagnated and blocked. This we know deep down happens because we are not allowing our energy to flow, because we are not allowing ourselves to flow.

As human and spiritual beings we constantly make and create new energy. We also as energetic beings take in, hold and absorb energy that is in and around us. When we understand this, we can learn to look at the different energy patterns that work through our energetic fields, boosting and deflating us, from the inside out and the outside in. With awareness we can start to notice how our energy can fluctuate according to how we are doing within ourselves, and that our physical energy is a direct result of our emotional, mental, and spiritual harmony and that nothing exists in isolation. Also, if not protected our energy can become diminished by surrounding ourselves with people and situations which drain us.

Understanding the World of Energy

Everything in our world has and is made up of energy. As such, everything works and lives within a vibration and a flow. Fire, air, water, wind, electricity, solar power, gas and satellite are all forms of energy that we have learned to understand and harness to live in the modern world. It is how our world communicates - through energy, and it is how we as human and spiritual beings communicate with ourselves, with each other, and with our world.

The same energy that runs through us and keeps us alive and breathing works also to foster energy in the entire universe, it's called *universal life force energy* and it is the power of all life force, including all planetary systems, star galaxies and the Earth itself, including every organism that lives within her energy field. We live in this world of energy and we ourselves are energy, as such we are open to giving and receiving energy constantly throughout our lives and our experiences.

In all our interactions we are picking up and communicating energy. Have you ever walked into a room filled with people and you instantly felt a certain type of energy, be it positive or negative, within that room? Or you bump into someone on the street and before you even speak to them and say "hello" you know how they are feeling. Somehow you sense and feel their energy.

The reason for this is that they are consciously or unconsciously sending out energy signals and you are consciously or unconsciously picking them up. This energy is coming from certain thoughts and feelings that is being held within their energetic field, otherwise known as an aura. This is the case for everyone - we all hold certain vibrations of energy in our fields that come from past, or present emotions and thoughts, and we are always communicating this energy on an energetic level, both internally and externally.

When we really begin to understand how we create energy and how it effects the human person and our Earth, we can begin to learn how to identify the different energy patterns that exist in and around our energetic fields. By clearing and re-balancing our energy system and unblocking trapped or stored energy that no longer serves our highest good, we can begin to open ourselves up more and more to our *True Self* and begin to live our lives in more balance, harmony and consciousness.

Healing our Lives, Past and All

As we begin to clear stagnated old energetic layers that cover us by healing our past we move our *Soul* forward, free to bring itself back to full consciousness and complete the healing it came here to do. In all our interactions and experiences there is the chance to heal, and become more and more aware, and this is the same for our past lives.

Past lives are also very significant for us, even if we are not consciously aware of them, for each past life holds an energy pattern and vibration from that life-time. These patterns and vibrations cover us like grids of light, holding shape in our auric fields. Each life gets marked on our *Soul journey*, with its deepest learnings and growth marked and recorded in the *Tree of Life*. Then on we go participating in our next life experience.

Taking responsibility for our energy means taking responsibility for our own healing and it means following our own inner guidance to bring about the changes we know we need to happen. Learning about energy healing and self-healing techniques can greatly help us to heal on emotional, mental, physical and spiritual levels by helping us to clear the past attachments that are causing us dysfunction and unease, allowing us to shine our true light out into the world.

This is the case for all our lifetimes, whether it is this one, or one thousands of years ago. Healing is healing, and energy is energy, and all blocked energy needs to be released back to the light. As we do, we reconnect with the *life force energy* of the universe, thereby boosting our energy fields back to healthy optimal levels so that we can bring about the healing, balance and peace that we so desire into our lives.

Healing of this kind helps to clear our energy fields of negative or imbalanced energy that is holding us back. Getting to the cause of the energy imbalance or block further acts to support us by gently allowing us to release the cause and therefore bring ourselves back to our natural state of free-flowing energy. Healing of this kind helps to foster an increased level of personal understanding, responsibility, and respect for *Self,* for others and all living things, including the planet we call home, Mother Earth.

Spirals of Light Connect Us to Source

Spirals of energy and light travel down from the Universe fueling us in this lifetime. Down it comes into our physical body and into our spiritual energy centers, otherwise known as chakra. This energy first enters through our **Soul Star** which is above our head, then down it comes, through our crown chakra in the center of the top of our head, here it travels through all our energy points… it moves down into our brow chakra, our throat chakra, and our heart chakra and connects with our **Spirit Star** which constantly glows as a beacon to our Soul.

Our spiritual energy continues passing down our *Body* into our solar plexus chakra, our sacral chakra and down into our root chakra, from here it moves down our body, through our legs, and out through the soles of our feet. Then it meets with our **Earth Star** just a few inches below our feet, grounding us to the Earth's energetic core.

This energy is continuously running through us and it works to energize our physical and spiritual bodies while we are here on Earth. It is also what connects us to our Spiritual or Higher Self and the source of all consciousness.

The Seven Major Chakra

A chakra is a Spiritual center that acts as a channel for life force energy and Soul consciousness within the physical and energetic body.

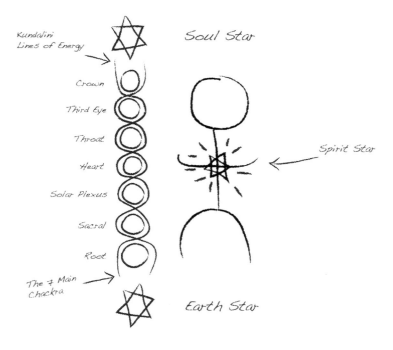

Charity Amy Murphy

Root: Our Root chakra is also known as the Base chakra. It is red in color and is responsible for our physical life force. It is associated with the feeling of security, safety, being grounded and manifesting the physical into being.

When it is open and flowing we feel safe and secure in our world. We have a strong grounding in ourselves and we stand tall and sure in our sense of identity. We know who we are, and we move forward conscious of each step we take.

When our Root chakra is blocked or stagnated, we can experience a lack of connection to the Earth and even to our own lives. We can feel a bit scattered or unbalanced. We can also feel insecure in our ability to remain safe and strong. It is our root to the physical world, so it is associated with anything to do with home, money, security and safety.

The root of the matter, ideas and therefore anything creative will need to have its essence (energetically) planted into the nourishment of the Earth, in order to spring into life. So too is anything that is manifested into the world of life.

And so, the heavens opened, and down a gleaming
ray of light shone the atoms of a new creation, deeper
and deeper it settled into the earth and from it sprang
a cluttering of new possibilities being born onto Earth.

Sacral: Our Sacral chakra is also known as our Creative chakra. It is orange in color and is responsible for our sense of creativity, our joy in life, and our ability to nurture and create, including new life.

When it is open and flowing we are open to the beauty of creation. We can nourish and provide a space for creative manifestations. We shine, emanating passion and pleasure into our lives, and we affirm our place in the world to be one of light and joy, as we work with the power of the universe in advancing that light throughout our interactions and manifestations in the world.

When our Sacral chakra is blocked or off balance we can often feel a sense of lowness or negativity. We can become despondent and fail to nourish ourselves in all ways, be it, physically, mentally, energetically or spiritually. We can fall into a darkness and forget to let ourselves shine. It is the light of life and has everything to do with reproduction, sexuality and the art of creative imaginings. It is the creative sphere.

And in the dark safety of the Mother, Earth, a light was born, and from it sprang all the elements of life. Here in the bosom of life, creativity itself was able to grow and develop in the nourishment of the human form. The heavens now had a place to shine, and in symphony with the universe was able to rejoice in the pleasure and joy of life. As you reap so shall you sow.

Solar Plexus: Our Solar Plexus chakra is yellow in color. It is the seat of our personal power, our self-worth and our peace center. It allows us to shine and excel in life. It helps us to assimilate, cleanse and purify the learning we receive in life.

When our Solar Plexus chakra is open and shining its brilliant glow of yellow light it helps us to shine our *True-Selves* out into the world with a gentle inner power. We are comfortable in our assertions of who we are, for we are at peace with who we are. Our ability to believe in ourselves comes from having worked through the learnings we have experienced in our life journey. It is the function of the Solar Plexus to assimilate our Soul story and therefore enable us to move forward with peace and strength in our identity of who we are. Having gained the insight, the lesson becomes the light we shine within.

When our Solar Plexus chakra is blocked or working through energies, we can feel a lack of personal power. We can be unsettled as the energy works through us finding its way forward into the light of our *Soul.* When our Solar Plexus chakra is cleansed, we are able to leave the old stories of who we thought we were behind, and step firmly into the light of our *True Selves*. We are able to allow our light to shine brightly, affirming our place in the world. As we glow, so too we grow, and it is our capacity to illuminate from within that builds the inner strength and joy of knowing where our true power comes from.

> *The Sun shone forth and illuminated the world in golden light, the grasses grew, and flowers sprang from the fertile Earth. The Sun brought light to the world and as it did Souls rejoiced in the miracle of life. Now they could step out of the dark, forevermore man would walk the Earth in the glow of light, shadowed in reflection by a shimmering moon. The Light would come to all.*

Heart: Our Heart chakra is green in color with a pink center. It is the seat of unconditional love, compassion, truth and grace. As spiritual beings our *heart* is the truth center of who we are. It allows us to feel, to connect and to love.

When our Heart chakra is open and flowing we experience a connection to the beauty and essence of life. We feel love and radiate it in all our interactions. We experience a deep and resting peace and we operate as healing vessels of love. Working through the issues of the heart brings great healing to a *Soul,* and it is the healing of such that brings true beauty to the world. Spreading compassion and grace, as we give and receive the energy of love. Un-biased, un-judging, un-wielding we keep moving ourselves forward centered in the grace of unconditional love.

When our Heart chakra is blocked or stagnated, we can often feel a sense of hopelessness. We can feel cut off from ourselves and our world and can question the purpose of who we believe we are. Emotional pain is quite often the cause of a blocked Heart chakra and everyone at one point or another will experience a mixed array of issues to do with the energy of love. How we heal and bring this energy to the light is our own path to walk and it is filled with insight and compassion for those who take the journey back into their *Soul*. Healing and expanding in understanding, the journey becomes clearer and the light becomes stronger.

> *As the Heart blossomed and grew, so too the Earth and all of life. A new way was here on the Earth and the path was filled with gifts from heaven. The Emerald sat in the vessel of man, and here it emanated its healing rays of light into the world. The Soul free to love, found solace in the pink hue of dawn.*

Throat: Our Throat chakra is sky blue in color and represents communication of all kinds. It is the bridging chakra from our Base, Sacral, Solar and Heart up to our Brow and Crown. Here we get to communicate our truth and give expression to who we are.

When our Throat chakra is open and flowing without any restriction or blocks, we speak our *Truth* into the world without effort. We speak with peace and assurance, and we are comfortable in honoring what we have to say in all our interactions.

When our Throat chakra is blocked it can mean we may find it hard expressing our true feelings and thoughts to others. The Throat chakra can be put out of balance because of experiencing the feeling of not being heard in your relationships. You could have experienced moments in your life when you felt your opinion didn't matter, or simply wasn't asked for or wanted, and so you got used to this. You may have been hurt emotionally and as a way of protection closed and hid your thoughts and feelings. You may have been bullied as a child or adult and didn't have the support to cope with it. You may even have had to fight to be heard, and therefore you didn't develop a healthy balance in how you communicate. It is a very sensitive chakra, and its balancing and healing eases the way for your true expression and *True Self* to come through into the world in peace.

> *And as the light shone through, man was able to direct his inner thoughts out into the world. His true feelings became a manner of expression, and the vibration of love was once more heard bellowing out across land and sea. The voice of God was present, and it lifted the Soul to hear its melodic healing sound.*

Third Eye: The Third Eye, or Brow chakra as it is also known, is indigo blue in color. A way of imagining it is like visualizing a twinkling dark blue night sky alight with sparkling stars shimmering in every direction. The Brow chakra has everything to do with the *Higher-Mind*. It is the gateway to our intuition and our ability to see psychically and think clearly.

When our Brow chakra is open and flowing we feel a direct connection to *our Higher-Mind*, the mind of our *Higher-Self*. We experience a strong sense of intuition and our thoughts are clear and streamlined. We can also develop our second sight, which is aided by our Third Eye - the spiritual connection to seeing in this world and the world of spirit.

When we have a blocked or stagnated Brow chakra, we can often find our thoughts run into one another. We may find it hard to have peace in our mind and may need help in trying to let it rest. We can also experience headaches, often caused by stress in our lives, and the mind being overburdened, quite literally stresses out with the pressure of having to think its way out all the time. Learning to allow your other parts of you, guide you, and help you, will ease the mind and allow it to flow. Cleansing the Brow chakra will help bring clarity and peace and will aid your Third Eye to open and thus guide you spiritually as your *Higher Self* speaks to your intuition bringing a gentle assurance to the path you are taking.

*The stars that are a twinkle and a flicker in the sky,
tell us of the deepest mystery of our lives. We look upon
the night sky, and call on heaven's door, to shine its
way right through us, so we may feel its Lore. The
Gods and Goddesses call us, and guide us on our way,
the few that listen follow, and come to pray each day.*

Crown: The Crown chakra is violet in color. It is our connection to Source and God Consciousness. Located at the top of our head it is the opening channel in which light and energy from the universe permeates our spiritual, emotional and mental being.

When our Crown chakra is open, flowing and spinning in harmony with the universe we experience a direct knowing and inner wisdom that comes from our openness to our *Higher Spiritual Self.* We are able to communicate with our spiritual guides and angels and we can receive direct communication from Source. There is a great peace and harmony that comes, and one can sense the wonder of life, and be at peace with God and the plan for consciousness unfolding on our planet.

When our Crown chakra is blocked or unbalanced we can feel cut off from our Higher Self. We can feel a sense of unknowing and confusion and we can wonder about our place in the world. Building a strong connection to your *Higher-Self* and Source will help to open your Crown and aid the development of your *Soul.*

*And when God spoke everyone listened, even if they
didn't think so. The vibration of the universe runs
through us. We are vessels of light and the light that
shines, shines inside all of us. Illuminating, healing
and guiding us home.*

The Aura: An aura is made up of the energy vibrations and depths of color that your chakra is producing. Each chakra holds an energetic frequency depending on the health and well-being of that chakra, and thus, our auras hold all the vibrations of all our chakra and are solely unique and dependent on how one's energy is working through their spiritual centers at specific moments throughout their lives.

Using Color and Sound in Energy Healing

If you want to help cleanse and clear your chakra, open your communication center and aid your own spiritual growth, you can begin by utilizing the healing and transformational power of sound and color to help you on your path.

Color Techniques: Imagine filling your chakra with the color it is associated with and start to tune into your own energy and see how it is doing. For example; The base chakra is associated with security, foundation, safety and grounding; if you are feeling low in your base chakra, you may like to wear red in that area to help boost its frequency.

Or say you feel that your throat chakra is blocked, a sign of this is feeling you are not able to express yourself freely, you may even get a sore or swollen throat; in this case you could try wearing a blue crystal necklace or a blue scarf or tie. Again, if you feel low in self-esteem, personal power or joy, then your solar plexus may need a boost, you could try wearing something yellow, eat lemons, even sit and look at a yellow wall, or simply sit and be in the sun and soak up its natural healing energy.

In other words, it does not matter what way you bring the color into your life the point is that you do. Know that whatever is going on in your life you can use the healing power of color to help boost and balance your energetic field by simply visualizing, noticing, wearing or surrounding yourself with the color you need at that time. It is also a nice practice to visualize your own chakra, from one to seven, and fill them with color and light every morning when you get up, and every night before you go to sleep.

Sound Techniques: Sound healing is very powerful and offers great peace and harmony to those who practice it. When using sound in healing, it is best to hum, tone or chant the vibrational note that one wants to build within ones' field. Often, we find that without being consciously aware we are already using sound for healing and the transformation of energy.

Toning, chanting, singing and humming are all forms and methods of releasing energy and also of transforming and shifting our levels of consciousness within ourselves. It is a very powerful way in which to connect with the deeper levels of your being.

We often find ourselves walking down the street or driving our car and we start to hum or sing a tune, suddenly we find that our mouth is opening, and melodic sound is coming out. People often say, "where did that come from?" And we answer, "I don't know, it just popped into my head." This is our unconscious or higher conscious *Self* picking up on the vibrational frequency we are needing.

Our spiritual guides will often, along with the angelic realm, send us messages and healing through music. It is a very powerful medium of healing and it has a way of lifting us out of darkness and into light in beautiful and pure ways. Anyone who has used the sacred healing properties of sound in a conscious way will know the resonance it has for the Soul and how it can lift us out of ego and into peace.

7 Chakra Mantra

This mantra is a great way to build up your energy and clear blockages. Try to visualize your chakra as you chant, starting with your root all the way up to your crown and then repeat it and get a nice rhythm going.

Lam, Vam, Ram, Yam, Ham, Aum, So-Ham.

When you are finished sit in silence and let the vibration resonate in and around your energetic field.

As a daily practice, it is a good idea to get into the habit of chanting or toning the chakra sounds in and throughout your day. Also use them in meditation to bring focus, stillness and expansion. They will help open you up to new levels of awareness within your *Self* and bring great healing to your *Soul*.

Protecting Your Energetic Field

Every day, focus on protecting and clearing your energetic field by clearing your chakra. Then imagine putting an energetic shield around your aura to keep you in your own energy.

A very simple way to protect your energy field is to simply imagine yourself sitting in an egg-shaped cocoon of light. See the light of your **Spirit Star** shine brightly out from your body, filling your cocoon with golden healing light. Imagine that all negative energy is dissolved by the light of your Spirit Star and see the beautiful golden light turn to a clear shimmering white light. Then visualize a blue steely silver lining forming a magnetic shield around your cocoon. This is your energy shield, and all you need to do to activate it is to see, feel, imagine, or call on it. If you ever feel uncomfortable or unsure of a situation, - simply call your Shield and it will appear, it is that simple. It will keep negativity out and healing energy in.

It is also good practice to get into the habit of calling your energy shield in the morning before you venture out into your day and again at night before bed. That way you begin to build up your energy internally by preventing your energy to leak out or become weak. Continuously see yourself surrounded by your energy shield and know that it is there, always surrounding you and keeping you safe and protected. Practice filling your cocoon with your different chakra colors and cleanse your aura with loving light.

Psychically cut energetic ties regularly, only negative energy will be released. All love will remain, because love is our truest vibration. Love is what is real.

Affirmation: I sit in my own healing light and shine
brightly - I engage my shield and so it is.

Go and learn more about your chakra, perhaps take a course in Reiki or other energy-based healing therapies. Go to your local library or book store and get some books on energy healing and practice some healing techniques at home.

Talk to your friends about what they know about energy and start to open your awareness to your own energy and how it works in your body. Start to notice how your thoughts and feelings affect your energy and also how the energy of others either bounces off you or attaches onto you, be it negative or positive. Remember to engage your energy shield regularly and work through your chakra colors, clearing and cleansing them one by one and filling them with light.

Journal time...

Take some time and think about an aspect from this chapter that stood out to you or resonated with you and write about it in your journal.

Exercise: Chakra Time

Draw your own chakra diagram and fill in each one with its associated color.

Healing in Body

Your Body is your Temple.
Look after your Body as it looks after you.
Look after you, and you look after your Body.

The Gift of Body

In life we house our *spiritual, emotional* and *mental* bodies in our human body. This body that we possess, that is a gift of form, is more than our vessel. It is our meter and our guide back to ourselves, and it will show us and guide us throughout our lives if we can learn to tap into its knowing.

Our bodies are magnificent, wondrous works of art and science that allow us to experience life and rejoice in all the pleasure of sense. We touch, we feel, we see, we hear, we smell, we sit, we stand, we run, we swim, we walk, we dance, we kiss, we make love, we caress, we hug, we laugh, we cry, we hurt, and we heal.

Your body does not need you to understand how it works, to work. Your body does not need you to know how to operate it, to make it work. Your body knows how to work, and it knows how to heal. It is an intricate vessel of innate beauty and intelligence beyond the capability of reason. Its simplicity lies in its complexity and having it as our temple allows us to experience life in all its greatness. It is a gift of body for the *Spirit* to experience life, and it is one we so often forget to honor and listen to.

We may not know it, but our bodies can be our messengers into how we are doing on an inner and deeper level, and our ailments; physical un-ease, dis-function and dis-ease are further extensions of us into form. They are often messages from our *Higher Self* to teach us and to show us what we need to heal and become aware of on a *Soul* level.

Energy Becomes Form

All throughout our lives we are striving to live a life without pain, yet often it comes into our lives and causes us discomfort. Why is this? Why do we sometimes have to suffer in health? Why does our body hurt? Why does our body weaken? So we can take notice of it! So we can start to look within, and uncover the meaning, the message, the cause, and learn how to heal it and in so doing heal ourselves.

Physical pain and ill health is one of the biggest attention grabbers our *Soul* can manifest in order to help us to change direction and go within. If taken seriously and used as the vehicle for change that our *Soul* is looking for, then the messages our body is showing us *can* work in getting us to focus and shift our attention to live more and more consciously and connect with our higher true selves.

Think about how you feel in your body when you are stressed. How does your body feel? It may ache, it may tire, it may stiffen up! Your body is reflecting you back to you. When we are stressed, we are tense in our thoughts and our body becomes tense.

Often our experiences of body are experiences of thought and emotion transferred into the physical form. It may be hard to understand at first, but our bodies are extensions of us, they are not us in totality. So, when we are suffering in body, we may actually be suffering on a deeper level within our *Soul*.

Emotional pain, guilt, feelings of lack, helplessness, grief, anger, sadness, mental anguish, thoughts of limitation and so on... are all transferred into our body to tell us and show us where we need to look and what we need to heal and let go of.

If we do not go in and heal the energetic cause then the stuck energy having no release, whether emotional or mental starts to form quite literally into physical form within the physical body. Hurt, sadness and emotional pain that has not been dealt with and healed start to solidify and turn into dis-ease.

Signs from Our Higher Self

Our body is our vessel, a vessel to experience human form and all the wonderful experiences that go along with it. Learning to tap into the messages our body gives us enables us to do the work on healing the problem *before* it escalates into the flashing neon sign which is screaming "slow down, you're going the wrong way."

Our *Body* gives us signposts to the areas in ourselves we need to look at. Some of the signposts are small like a sore hand, or a headache, and sometimes, just sometimes they come to us in a big flashing neon sign, like cancer or a heart attack. If we ignore the small signs they eventually build and grow inside us until eventually it gets to the stage where we can ignore them no longer and we are forced to take action.

Think about it logically. If you're your *Higher Self* and you're trying to get your attention about something say pretty important, like for instance your *Soul's* life journey, or your *Soul's* spiritual growth, what things do you think you might use to try and get your attention? You may whisper in your ear, and try to gently guide you to make certain choices or decisions. You may arrange situations of opportunity to help you take the right path. You may even put diversions in place around your bad decisions to help stir you in the right direction.

What happens if you, being the clever person that you are, find a way around those diversions? Or, you show yourself how strong you are and push right through them. What then do you think your *Higher Self* might do? What can it do? At this point your *Soul* is getting very concerned and it knows it may have to take drastic action to get your attention. Your Soul is always trying to guide you through this life and that is exactly what it is going to do, even if you're not aware it is.

Say you are now going in completely the wrong direction; you're not listening to the whispers of your *Soul* or taking notice of the signs that are being placed down beside you for you to see and take notice of. In this situation you might find that you develop a series of illnesses, or dis-eases. You may even pull a ligament or break a bone. In other words, something may manifest in your life physically that makes you *have* to slow down. You may find your old routines are disrupted and you have more and more time to think and be with yourself. More and more time to reflect, to go within and to start to heal and connect with the teachings of your *Soul*.

Why? So we can learn to slow down, learn how to connect with our *Soul* and to be brought back into our *Hearts*. It is always about healing, and your *Soul* and your *Higher Self* will guide you to grow and heal just as you wished to do entering into this great life experience.

Our body is a tool for self knowledge, self care and it is the compass of our *Soul*. See where it is it may be pointing you and then go and discover the voyage it has planned for you. Do so with a sense of adventure and exploration, and find new territories within yourself. Become your own private eye, do your own detective work and then start putting the puzzle together to see what it is your *Body* and your *Soul* are trying to show you.

Discovering the meta-physical reasons behind our illnesses allows us to take the lead in our own health care. Understanding the mental and emotional patterns that are behind our illnesses gives us the space in which we can go in and heal the cause from the inside out. This should, of course, be done in conjunction with professional medical science and care and never instead of. There is room for both and each has its role in our lives.

On an energetic level - over time, if we do not heal and clear the stagnated or blocked energy that comes from past experiences then they begin to layer over each other energetically and clog us up. The more severe the dis-ease or dis-function we are experiencing, the longer we have been holding it in our field. Our bodies are energy and energy has patterns, breaking patterns means healing them and letting them go.

Unearthing and understanding the mental or emotional cause of the physical dis-ease or dis-function we are experiencing allows us to get to its root so that we can lift it out and heal the wound. Wounds of all kinds, physical, mental and emotional, past or present all carry vibrations. These vibrations hold energy frequencies that are carried in and around our energetic field. Learn to feel with your *Body*, learn to listen to it, learn to connect with it and learn to honor it. It will show you the way back to yourself if you listen.

Exercise: Tapping Back into My Body to Know and Heal

Take a few moments and think about all the ailments, illness, injuries and physical dis-functions you have experienced in your life so far. You may want to go back over your life map to help rejog your memory. Think back as far as you can and write them down.

Listing My Experience of Body
eg: I broke my left arm - June 1982 age 8. I got the flu – October 2014 age 39.

_____

_____

_____

_____

_____

_____

_____

Physical Ailment: - Now take a step back and look at the ailment or injury itself. *What exactly is or was the problem? What is the function of the body part affected? In what way does it or did it restrict or hinder you?*

Describing My Ailment - Explain it in your own words...

_____

_____

_____

Explain how it happened or the circumstances that led to it...

_____

_____

_____

Explain how you were feeling in yourself before it occurred...

_____

_____

_____

What was the outcome, diagnosis or recovery program...

_____

_____

_____

How did this affect your life...

_____

_____

_____

What feelings did you experience as a result...

_____

_____

_____

What issues has it made surface within you...

_____

_____

_____

Learning the Soul Lesson

All our experiences are a part of our _Soul lesson_ and it is only by going through them that we can indeed learn from them. When we learn the _Soul_ lesson it sinks into our being, and from that absortion we are free of it. The lesson stays, and we shift up in consciousness, healing and understanding.

We can then lift off the energetic frequencies caused by the pain and trauma, leaving only the light, loving energy that accompanies the _Soul_ lesson. In turn, we are more solid and in our selves, while also being lighter and brighter.

Our _Higher Self_ may pick the lessons for us to learn, but the lessons are not who we are. We need to learn from them and then set them free. For we are our _Highest Vibrations_, in _Spirit_ and in _Soul_, this is our true essence.

When you get to the root cause or _Soul_ lesson, actively set about bringing healing back to your whole _Self_, inside and out. Thank your _Body_ for being your messenger, thank the lesson and then set it free and work consciously to bring about the change that is needed for you to truly mend and heal. Learning to heal our past and our present frees the Body to flow without restriction.

So sit back into yourself and really connect and ask yourself what can you learn from your experiences of Body. What have you been holding on to, either on a conscious or unconscious level. What emotions are held deep inside, trapped and forgotten about? What can you now let go of. What can you now heal ? What is your _Soul_ trying to show you? How can you use these experiences to further the development of your _Soul Journey_, and how can they help you to open and heal your _Heart_ even more?

In order to bring true healing to ourselves we need to learn to forgive and set free what no longer serves us. Ask yourself what do you now need to let go of? What do you need to face? What do you need to accept? What do you need to forgive? What can you finally release and bless and set free? Total and absolute deep honest reflection is needed for this exercise. Take your time and allow yourself to gently free your *Soul* from past pain, guilt, grief, anger or fear. Hold yourself in a place of love.

Exercise: Releasing the Past with Love and Light

Before you begin find yourself a quiet place and sit with yourself a while. Then pull your *Self* inside your *Body* and connect with it's knowing. Imagine a white light entering the top of your crown, spiriling down your centre, moving in and around your spinal coloum, and coming out the soles of your feet, traveling down into the ground below you reaching deep into the center of the Earth.

See yourself in your mind's eye filled with healing white light, imagine this light illuminating every cell in your *Body*. Sit in this light and call in your *Soul*, asking it to guide you in discovering the messages your *Body* has stored for you.

Then affirm - *"I call on my Higher Self and ask for guidance to know, learn, accept and heal from the Soul lesson that has manifested in my life for me to grow with. I fill myself with love and light and ask that my communication center be cleansed and cleared so that I may be open to my own inner wisdom and all that I have to teach myself."*

Affirmation: I listen to my body as it shows me where to look and heal.

You will have to really sit with this and allow yourself to reach deep inside and ask your *Body* and your *Higher Self* to show you what it wants you to learn. Ask it to show you how to discover its deeper *Truth*, its meaning and why it has manifested.

What does it force you to look at? What message does it hold for you?
What is it calling for to be released and healed?

What is my body trying to tell me?

_____

_____

_____

How or why has this dis-function, illness or dis-ease manifested into my life?

_____

_____

_____

Where did it really come from?

_____

_____

_____

What emotional or mental block is it related to?

_____

_____

_____

What do I need to face and heal?

_____

_____

_____

What do I need to accept?

_____

_____

_____

What do I need to forgive, release or set free?

_____

_____

_____

What am I learning deep inside?

_____

_____

_____

What is my Soul showing me?

_____

_____

_____

Can I love and honor my Body and give thanks for all it does?

_____

_____

_____

Affirmation: I now let the past go and step firmly into my Now - I AM at peace - I AM healthy, healed and whole - I AM My I AM Self. I AM My Highest Vibration.

The Act of Self Awareness

Learning through self-awareness to be in touch with our feelings and thoughts helps us to sense our own energy fields and foster it in positive ways, thereby facilitating us to live more and more consciously and experience and enjoy all our moments, in health, and in strength. Having a solid and strong energy foundation allows you to go forward in your life peacefully, balanced, healthy and whole.

After the life lesson has been learned, and your *Soul* has moved through the teachings and expansion of healing that it needed, it is then time to shift the more denser and heavier energy that may have accumulated from the experience back to the light. Sometimes old energy needs a helping hand in being released. You can use meditation, visualization and energy healing practices to aid you in your spiritual journey of discovery and awareness. Doing so will help you open up your own inner wisdom, so that you can allow the teachings go where they need to go, and free you up, so you can accept the healing that has accompanied it.

In other words, maybe you have done all the internal work and identified the root cause, learnt the lesson, healed the issue and brought yourself back to a place of peace. Yet you may notice that the stagnated energy that came from the experience or *Soul* lesson is still hanging around your energetic field. In this instance you need to lift and clear the old energy and release it back to the light. Every time you do this you will allow a healing space to emerge in which you will move and shift up to new levels of healing and awareness.

Always be mindful that there is a divine timing in everything, including healing, so let your *Higher Self* guide you and don't rush your way through. Take time to meditate and learn to trust your intuition as you move forward, conscious of each and every step you take.

The visualization that follows will help you start the process of clearing your energetic field, thereby enabling you to balance your Mind, Body, Spirit and emotions to bring clarity, peace, joy and harmony to your *Soul*.

Visualization: Clearing the Block with Light and Love

Start by connecting with your *Higher Self* and ask your *Soul* and your *Spiritual Guides* to ascertain that the *Soul lesson* in its *Truth* and *Light* be placed in the *Tree of Life*. Then quite simply see yourself being filled with *healing golden light* as it is poured down from your *Soul Star* into the crown of your head. See the light continue to fill your body and energetic field, until you become one with that light and you sense all negative or blocked energy has been transmuted back to the light.

Then visualize your chakra - *crown, brow, throat, heart, solar, sacral and root.* See them spinning in harmony and fill them with their associated color - *violet, indigo, blue, green, yellow, orange and red...*until they are all shining; a beautiful luminous symphony of light.

Engage your shield, and then follow on and make a personal affirmation, releasing the old energy block and reaffirming your *Self* filled with love and light.

Affirmation: I now release _____ and set it free, my energy field is cleansed, cleared and healed and I sit in my own circle of healing light. I AM my Highest Vibration.

Journal time...

Take some time and think about an aspect from this chapter that stood out to you or resonated with you and write about it in your journal.

Exercise: Nourishment Plan

In your journal write out three ways you can add nourishment to your body. What nutrient-rich foods can you add to your diet? What juices could you make? How much water do you drink each day? Think about how you look after your body right now and how you can improve on it and then actively practice putting your ideas into operation in your every day.

Exercise: Vitality and Movement

How happy is your body? Does it get to move and stretch enough each day? In your journal write down what exercise you currently do. Then ask your body what it might like to do. Does it like to swim? Walk, cycle, hike, dance, run, stretch? Take some time and tune into your body and see if it is getting all it needs. Look up some local classes or retreats, join a club or meet up group. Maybe try something completely new, something you've always been curious about, then make a plan and schedule in some vitality time for yourself. Your body will be so happy!

Family: Healing the Bonds that Brought Us Here

*The Vibration of life is within us and we
live, love and evolve through the stories we are born into.*

Discovering My Family Tree

This chapter is concerned with taking you back in time to discover the family line that you have been born into. What patterns are running through your family's genetic line? What has been the story of your entry into the world? Who are your parents and what is their story? What ancestral healing, strengths and qualities can you foster in your life to carry through, and what healing needs still to be done.

Reflecting on your entry into the world and carrying out an internal journey of your own family history and experiences will help to give you a deeper sense of your chosen life lessons, and how you fit in to assisting your family complete cycles for healing. It is like looking at an island and then pulling back and seeing that this island sits in a sea surrounded by other islands that make up a grander and greater picture than you once thought. You also learn that each island has its own story to tell, and that they all exist to make up your world and you theirs.

Family Life

Growing up in any family involves multiple arenas of juxtaposed emotions to do with unity, separation and concealment of *Self.*

Families of all kinds (loving, solid, dysfunctional, erratic, damaging and conventional) all make up the norm. Everybody experiences moments of hurt and moments of joy within their family life, and all of us are challenged to learn and grow, to accept ourselves as individuals and to heal the bonds that brought us here.

It does not matter which family *type* we get labeled with, or which category of childhood we believe we belong to - happy, sad, lonely, overcrowded, normal, perfect! All family experiences teach us and see us go through a process of contradictions and healing. These experiences of family are offerings, vantage points in which we get to learn and grow. They are a part of our *Soul* lesson.

We seek, and we mark, and we continue certain patterns until we learn what they have to teach us. We do so in conjunction with other *Souls* who are also on their journey of life, and we all fit perfectly together, teaching each other along the way. It is all about growth and development, and it is always done in love; even when we can't imagine it is, it is. It is the love of one *Soul* for another that allows it to enter into this life agreement and vice versa.

There are exciting developments in the field of epigenetics which show that we can alter the dynamics of our genes in positive ways, for they are no longer seen as stagnant, but fluid and mutable. Science is showing us that *genetic memory* is passed down our blood lines and that we inherit the positive and negative energies of our ancestors for at least three generations. It is the capacity of one generation to pass on its learning for the next, and what is becoming evident in this field of study is that we have the power and ability to alter and modify our genes with our mindset and environment.

No longer do we have to accept blindly the patterns of the past, but we can actively take the lead in enhancing the family line we have been born into. This knowledge is changing the goal posts for the development of human existence. It is firmly and coherently placing us in the forefront of our own lives and aligning us with the knowledge and power to positively enhance the world by healing our own *Self* and therefore by extension, the world.

FAMILY MAP
Use the chart below to map out your family tree

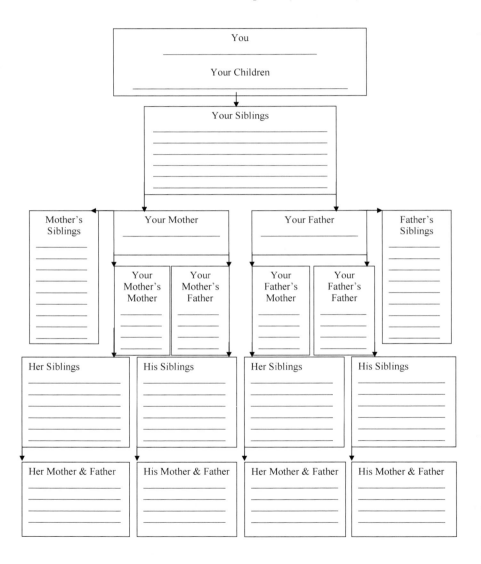

You

Your Children

Your Siblings

Mother's Siblings

Your Mother

Your Father

Father's Siblings

Your Mother's Mother

Your Mother's Father

Your Father's Mother

Your Father's Father

Her Siblings

His Siblings

Her Siblings

His Siblings

Her Mother & Father

His Mother & Father

Her Mother & Father

His Mother & Father

Charity Amy Murphy

Use the exercises in this chapter to gain a deeper understanding of not just your story, but also your family's story, and see if you can see how your island makes up their world just as much as they make up yours.

And Then Along Came Me

On a *Soul* level we come to each other to assist in each other's growth and we choose our families based on what life lessons our Soul wishes to learn. Each family has specific experiences both as a group and individually for each family member, and no two family members will experience their family in the exact same way. And while we will all have similar experiences, we will also all have our own very personal experiences that are ours to feel and grow with.

Use your *Family Map* as a guide and write down where you came in on your family tree. When and where were you born? Who were you born to? What family members were prominent in your early life? How did your life begin? What was your childhood like, your upbringing, your experience of family life, and your relationships within your family? What was going on in your family when you came along?

Exercise: And then Along Came Me

You can start by saying, "I was born at ... on ... to ...

_____

_____

_____

_____

_____

_____

_____

_____

_____

_____

(Continue in your journal or on a separate sheet if needed)

Charity Amy Murphy

When you are finished, don't read what you wrote quite yet, just let it sit a while. Sometimes this can be the first time that we get to release this part of our story. Each time we open a dialogue with our past we offer a new space for inner emotional imprints to come out for healing. How do we heal? With awareness, with compassion, and with *Soul*. When you feel ready, read what you wrote and bless your story and the story of how you came into the world.

My Parents Before Me

In this next exercise we get to flip the deck and change the story by switching perspective. Go back and take a look at your **Family Map** and look at it *before* you came along. What was it like to be a part of this family? What are the stories of your parents? Who were they?

Take a step back from your life as you have learnt it to be and write the lives of your parents. This will entail you looking at their life not from your eyes but rather from theirs. To do so you will have to move yourself away from seeing yourself as being their child and write from a place where they are the center of their world.

You were born to two people, separate in their own right, but brought together in their own lives to make life - You. Step back and start to see them as a person in their own right. Allow yourself to really try and understand their life journey, their pain and their joy, their accomplishments, their sacrifices, their hopes and dreams and how they developed into the people they became as adults. See them from a tiny baby born to two people (your grandparents), see their childhood, their upbringing and their own personal journey.

Exercise: Their Stories

My Mother's Story:

Start with your Mother. Some questions you could ask yourself might be...who was she before she became pregnant with you? What had been her life? What was her childhood like? What was her relationship like with her parents, her brothers, her sisters? What were her wants and desires for herself in life? How did she meet your Father? What was their relationship like? What age was she when she had you? What was going on in her life when you came along? What is her life now? What has been her journey?

My Mother...

_____

_____

_____

_____

_____

_____

_____

_____

_____

_____

_____

_____

_____

_____

_____

_____

_____

_____

_____

_____

_____

_____

_____

_____

_____

_____

_____

_____

_____

_____

_____

_____

_____

_____

_____

_____

_____

_____

_____

_____

_____

_____

_____

_____

_____

_____

_____

_____

(Continue in your journal or on a separate sheet if needed)

My Father's Story:

Next do the same for your Father. Who was he before your Mother got pregnant with you? What had been his life? What was his childhood like? What was his relationship like with his parents, his brothers, his sisters? What were his wants and desires in life? How did he meet your Mother? What was their relationship like? What age was he when you were born? What was going on in his life when you came along? What is his life now? What has been his journey?

My Father...

_____

_____

_____

_____

_____

_____

_____

_____

_____

_____

_____

_____

_____

_____

_____

_____

_____

_____

_____

_____

_____

_____

_____

(Continue in your journal or on a separate sheet if needed)

Exercise: The Generation Game

Now it is the time to go further back in your family history and do some detective work. Start by looking back on everyone's life story, really absorbing what it all means. Go back to your *Family Map* and try to answer as many questions as you can for each family member.

Name(s) and known as:	
Relationship to you:	
Born: Time, Date, Place:	
Parents names in full:	
Siblings names in full:	
Married: To, Place, Date:	
Children's names in full:	
Characteristics: Personality:	
Passions: Interests: Hobbies:	
Occupation:	
Struggles:	

Achievements:	
Funny Story:	
Sad Story:	
Favorite Story or Favorite Memory:	
Their Story: - upbringing - childhood - education - interests - adult years - career - love - family life - illness - passing over	

(Use this as a template and continue on within your journal for each family member)

Exercise: Putting the Generational Pieces Together

Family healing work is very cleansing, and it offers a space for deep and profound shifting to occur within ourselves, and therefore within the very blood lines that we have been born into. Recap on what came out of *The Generation Game*. Look at the family bloodlines starting with your mother, then her mother, her father, her father's father etc. Then follow the same sequence for your father's side. Use the space below to pick out significant events as you take note of them. See if you can spot the same lessons, or issues coming up again and again, asking to be recognized and brought into the light.

Following the Blood Lines Down

Use this space to take note of what stands out within your family line.

Mother's Blood Line	Father's Blood Line	Both Blood Lines
_____	_____	_____
_____	_____	_____
_____	_____	_____
_____	_____	_____
_____	_____	_____
_____	_____	_____
_____	_____	_____
_____	_____	_____
_____	_____	_____
_____	_____	_____
_____	_____	_____
_____	_____	_____

When you are finished look back over and take note of any similarities or patterns carried over, through or between families. See if you can puzzle any pieces together to see how family lines can intermingle for specific reasons, bringing people together to form and heal patterns perhaps manifested generations before.

Take a moment here and look back and see what negative aspects might have been running through your family line. What are the patterns and programs that are carrying blocks or hindering the growth of those carrying them? What patterns are calling for healing? Calling for transformation? Take a good look and write it all down, marking the pattern, the family member (or members) who have experienced them, and the current status of the pattern.

Negative Pattern:	Family Member(s):	Status of Pattern:
_____	_____	_____
_____	_____	_____
_____	_____	_____
_____	_____	_____
_____	_____	_____
_____	_____	_____
_____	_____	_____
_____	_____	_____
_____	_____	_____
_____	_____	_____
_____	_____	_____
_____	_____	_____

Now look at what strengths your ancestors hold for you? What characteristics and personalities stand out to you? What are their essences that resonate with you? What positive strengths and character needs to be celebrated and honored in your family? What people in your family bring hope and show compassion, courage, love, strength, beauty, honor and joy? What are the qualities and strengths you wish to bring forward in your family lineage:

Person:	Strength/Character:	Quality/Essence:
_____	_____	_____
_____	_____	_____
_____	_____	_____
_____	_____	_____
_____	_____	_____
_____	_____	_____
_____	_____	_____
_____	_____	_____
_____	_____	_____
_____	_____	_____
_____	_____	_____

With the information gathered take some time to reflect and then write your ancestors' stories for them as best as you can. You may want to take some time and talk with other family members about what they may know about your family's story, the story of your blood line and all of those that have shared it with you down the line.

What are the similarities that are carried through, over or in between family lines? Whose name lives on in others? What interests, personalities, essences, strengths, weaknesses, ailments, talents, skills and stories can you see being passed on and through your family? Remember to keep an eye out for patterns and similarities among your family group and see if you can spot opportunities for life lessons marked along your family's path.

The Story of My Ancestors...

_____

_____

_____

_____

_____

(Please continue in your journal or on a separate sheet if needed)

Healing the Patterns of the Past

Raising one's consciousness can not only help heal your present, it can also help clear and heal blocks within bloodlines that have been running in and through your family history for generations. Are there any negative patterns that may have come from those before you, that have been passed down the genetic line? Patterns that now you have the opportunity to transform within yourself.

Everything can be healed, and everybody has the ability to shift their family forward through their own healing. Is there anything you can change or heal in order that you don't carry negative family patterns down to your own children and children's children? Can you identify one or two such patterns currently running within you? Areas of your *Self* that now you would like to heal?

Affirmation: I bless my family line with Love and Light
and I call on the Truth and Beauty of my ancestors
to shine brightly within my Heart. I honor those that
came before me and all those that are yet to come.

Meditation: Healing with the Golden Light and Violet Ray

This meditation will help heal negative patterns that are running in you, or others.

To Begin, pick a pattern that you would like to bring healing to.

Now imagine a ball of *golden light* is in front of you and place the pattern in the golden light and ask for it to become that light. See the golden light envelope it and transform it in healing energy.

Now see the person (whether it is yourself or someone else) with whom the pattern is running through, stand before you and visualize them in a bubble of white light. Then call on the *violet ray* to enter the persons bubble and pour its healing light into the crown of their head, down their spine and into each Chakra illuminating and transforming any, and all negative and dense energetic pockets that are trapped within them. See the light of their *Spirit star* glow a powerful bright golden light from within filling their entire bubble.

See the person pick up the golden bubble of light that the pattern had been placed in and see them bring this golden bubble into their own golden bubble. The two become one and in the healing golden light they are healed and set free. Send a blessing and give thanks.

> *Affirmation: I now clear and heal all that came before me and in so doing move my family linage forward: balanced and free and open to the Truth of conscious awareness.*

Journal time…

Take some time and think about an aspect from this chapter that stood out to you or resonated with you and write about it in your journal.

Exercise: My Family and Me

Start a section in your journal and answer the following questions as best as you can:

1. What do you think your family is teaching you on your journey?
2. What do you think you are teaching your family on their journey?
3. Can you pick out the main teachings that exist within your family?
4. Can you see the areas that need healing, that need transforming?

5. Can you step back from yourself and be a witness to your family's story?
6. Can you now move your family forward in healing by healing yourself?
7. Can you see the love within your family that needs nourishment and celebrating?

Exercise: Family Map Album

It is a nice idea following on from all of this, to make a Family Map Album or Wall Mount and give a space to each family member, telling a bit of their story for them as it was handed down to you. You can include photos or drawings and even collage images of their favorite things. Perhaps you could bring your family together in a group project and work together in putting your family tree together, then celebrate your heritage and cherish the qualities of those who came before you.

Chapter 10

Living in Spirit, Living in Soul

There is a world of Spirit existing in this world
that some find hard to comprehend.
Yet its existence is as real
as the air we breathe.

We Are All the Same

We come to this life school with the hope to be shown how to
be free in *Spirit*, what we forget so often is that we already are
Spirit. Remembering this is what ultimately makes the human
experience joyous. Accepting your own divinity and seeing it in
all around you and in your everyday experiences brings about
a shift so transcending that you move from fear to love and
you begin to see a world of possibilities that are not based in
illusion but in vision. You begin to see a world not from inside
your head but from inside your *Heart*, and you learn that all of
us are connected, every single one of us.

We are all on our own journey and at the same time we are
all on the same journey. People come in and out of our lives
from the moment we are born until the moment we pass on.
We come together for moments of joy, moments of conflict,
moments of sorrow and moments of love.

We live, and we share lives with people, we experience
fleeting glances and emotional encounters. All throughout
our lives people enter it and alter it, some in simple ways and
some so profoundly that it brings about a shift that transcends

our very being and we are moved in ways we didn't know possible.

Meeting Those on Your Journey

The people we meet at different points in our life are also on their journey, and our interaction with them works to assist their *Soul* bring about change in them also. We meet at certain times to share, to experience and to grow, and these parts of your and their journey are just that, parts. This time of contact you spend with one another, this meeting, this interaction is not the whole of them, it is a moment in their life that they too are going through, that they are allowing you to see. Remember, you see this part of them through the filters you have devised around them, and you will only see what they and you allow to be seen, nothing more.

You can attempt to guess or assume who this person is, but you would only be playing with your ego and manifesting an illusion. You do not know the inner thoughts of this person; you do not know their inner pain, their secrets, their hopes, their insecurities, their desires and their joys. You did and do not experience their obstacles on their life journey. You did and do not have to overcome their life lessons, you do not think with their head or feel with their heart, and you do not live in their body.

What you do know is that their *Spirit* exists just as much as yours, and that they, like you, are living a life here on Earth and learning just as you are. The fact that you have met means that there is some sharing to be done between you both, keep this in your conscious awareness and bring it forward from time to time to see if you can feel the undercurrents of *Spirit* developing in and around you. Learn to let ego go and feel instead with your *Soul*. Hold everyone in love and allow the love of your *Soul* to emanate out and touch the *Souls* around you, healing and expanding as you do.

Keep in mind that the time that you meet is just one point in both your and their life, it is but a moment of passing that you will both encounter, and it will affect you in differing ways. Each of your *Spirit* giving and receiving, each somehow marking a shift in each other's journey. You may have lessons to learn or lessons to teach, you may have gifts to pass on or to be awakened within. Know throughout your encounters that you meet to share a part of your journey with them and them also with you.

Keeping an Open Heart

Keeping yourself and basing yourself in a *State of Spirit* will enable you to sway away from ego driven judgment and separation and will prevent a mind only analysis. Allowing yourself to remain centered in your own spiritual divinity opens up channels of love and gratitude for the experiences of life and thus enables us to see our life experiences and those around us with compassion, understanding and love. Remember that the times we spend with each other, short, long or intermittent are moments of sharing, moments of giving and moments of receiving, and that we are always learning, and we are always growing.

Each one of us is learning to know and live with ourselves in all of our moments, and the paths that bring us together are pin points in time, book markers in our chapters of life, everyone you meet is going through their life lessons too. Keep an open heart and give what you can to each you meet for at the end of it all we are all the same and we give to others what we give to ourselves. Give love out and you will receive love in, live with a heart of love and you will live your life in love. Peace, joy and happiness are not outside of ourselves, they are inside waiting to be let out and shared.

Feeling and Living in Spirit

Stilling your mind and opening your heart are all part of living in Spirit. Reconnecting with your divine Source enables you to carry out your life plan with greater clarity and understanding. As we learn to tap into our senses and feelings and connect them with opportunities and life lessons, we move forward in reclaiming our destiny. It is all about learning to see what is right there in front of us.

Observe your hunches, your feelings, your thoughts, your knowing and your own inner guidance, for it is your *Higher Self* and it is trying to guide you on your *Soul Journey*. All the information we need, we already know, we just need to learn to listen, to feel, to sense and to see. We need to bring the unconscious to the conscious and stop being afraid of what we will find in the depths. There is no magic wand and there are no tricks or quick fixes. But there is potential for real and lasting healing, and it comes from learning to see what is, or has been, and heal the attachments that pull and keep you trapped.

Living Without Judgment

Living in *Spirit* is living in understanding, it is living with an open heart, it is living in compassion and it is living without judgment. It is living in your own divine personal power and it is radiating these out to the world around you. When we radiate we illuminate, and when we show and feel compassion for each other, those around us energetically pick it up. They sense it and they feel it on many levels, it touches them and they in turn take it in and radiate it back out.

When we live with an open heart we send out pure love to all those around us, it can't help but radiate out and touch the hearts of everyone we come into contact with. When hearts feel love they learn to soften and open, and they themselves radiate out the love that lies within them.

When we live our lives without judgment we acknowledge our divineness and it radiates outwards and touches the Souls of all those around us, touching their Spirits which rejoice in its recognition of its *Self*. When we live our lives in understanding we recognize that we are all the same, we all come from the same

Source and we are all here to learn and to live and to share and to grow. By living our lives in understanding we delete the need for competition, for jealousy, for bitterness, for fear and for pain.

By living in understanding we comfort, we support, we nurture, we love. For when we live in *Spirit* we reach above, we reach below, and we reach within, in to ourselves, into each other and into our Source, yours, mine and the entirety of *Soul Consciousness*. We spread, we multiply, and we radiate.

The light of our Spirit shines brightly if we let it. It shines inside each one of us, all we need do is recognize it and it will radiate so brightly that it will illuminate our entire world, spreading compassion, love and understanding. From this we will find peace; peace of Heart, peace of Mind and peace of Soul.

All throughout our *Soul journey* we are moving and evolving and learning and transcending. It is the journey of a *Soul* to bring itself through its experiences while always maintaining to reach its full conscious state and return to its natural spiritual dimension of love and light. For in truth we are *energy*, and we are *light*, and at our most heightened state we are simply beings of love and light, spreading out, expanding and joining back together again.

Facing the Mortality of Human Existence

The sacred Spirit that is within never dies, there is no death, there is simply a transition of form to formlessness, a return to Source. As *Spirit* living a human life, we come at the end of this wonderful journey we call life, to a space where we reconnect fully with our *Soul Self* and complete the steps of healing that we came here to do. It is the *Soul* of a person that lives on. When we can stop being afraid of death and dying, then we can stop being afraid of life and living.

In the last days, months, and hours of our lives here on Earth it is hoped that while our bodies may become weak and we prepare to take our departure, that our *Spirit* has once again become strong. And that before we take our leave of this life we have re-connected with who we are as a *Soul and* are at peace with all that we have been.

It is the spiritual dimension of a person that you must learn to accustom yourself with, for that is all there really is. The essence of each person continues, and you carry the life journey of your Soul as you go from life to death and death to life. If a strong bond has occurred between Souls, then it is most likely that you will meet again in the next life, in a different time, a different body and a different life experience. When you meet you will know somewhere deep inside that this person and you have a connection. That there is some bond of love between you, and that you have met before - some other time, some other place, some other reality. It is the *Soul* that you will recognize, it is the *Soul* that you will meet again.

Life Lessons - Miracle Shall Follow Miracle and Wonders Shall Never Cease

Everyone is here for the same reason, to experience life and to grow with those experiences. Everyone has a past, a present and a future, and everyone has hopes, desires and fears. Everyone feels joy and every one of us feels pain. And everyone, every single one of us, has something we want to do and accomplish with our lives, something to pass on, something our *Higher Self* chose before entering this lifetime.

The experiences you encounter on your journey are your lessons in *Heart.* We all come here to learn and to teach and to leave something unique behind and it is a gift to be able to enrich the world and everyone in it by sharing with it your life lessons, your acts of faith and your experience of life.

To share these experiences is a chance for you to give back what you have learned, to reveal your life lessons and your *Truth* honestly. Sharing in this way will help foster a discovery of *Truth* in others, so that they can further grow in compassion, unity and love.

A Parable on Passing Over: A man lies in a hospital bed. His daughter lies at his feet crying. The man becomes quiet and still in himself. He touches his daughter's hand not looking at her, and whispers softly, "I didn't listen, I didn't see." His daughter lifts her head. She searches her father's face, "what didn't you see, what do you mean?" Her father stares ahead blankly, lost in a haze of memories. "I didn't look at my life, I didn't stop to see who I truly was," he turns to face his daughter. "I have spent my whole life running from who I am, and now I feel that maybe I am starting to know, starting to realize… and it is my time to leave, to go." The man pauses, his eyes become soft, gentle even, he looks out the window and sighs a slow quite breath, "I am leaving, Sarah." He turns to face his daughter who has a tear falling down her left cheek. "I'm leaving, and I don't know who I am." His daughter lifts her father's hand to her face; she stares into his eyes, connecting deep within his Soul. "I know who you are." She rests her cheek on his hand and looks further into his eyes, "I know who you are… and I will see you again dear Father, I will see you again." Her father sees the love deep within his daughter's eyes and peace comes to him. He closes his eyes and in a moment of breath he has passed knowing who he is, knowing who we all are, knowing that love is all there really is.

Exercise: Reflections: Preparing to Die - Learning to Live

The next step involves a leap in your imagination and a going in to your *Heart* and *Soul*. Imagine you have reached the end of this lifetime on Earth and you are waiting to pass on to your next journey. Before you go you have been asked to leave a message to your loved ones and the world you are leaving behind. It is hoped that your message will enrich the lives of those still here and help them in their journeys and the journey of the planet and the human race.

You sit here now, and you look back on your life. It has been a good life, you have lived it well and with much love. You have had struggles, you have had heartache, and you have had many,

many beautiful and enriching moments throughout your life. You take this opportunity now to really reflect on what it has all meant to you. How do you feel?

Sit with this a while and really feel it.

Take into your consciousness all of your experiences of *Heart* and refresh yourself with your life path. Reflect back on your life and think of all the things you have learned, all the things you have done, all the things you have been a part of, all the loves you have experienced and shared with others, think of all the pain you felt, and think of all the joy; think of your most precious moments, the times when you have truly felt alive, the times when you have felt the deepest of love and the gentlest of peace in your *Heart*, the times when you have touched *Spirit* and lived in your *Soul*.

Think, feel and be.

Then think about what you can pass on to those you love. How can you use your life lessons to help heal and teach your children, and your children's children? How can your life experiences be a gift back to your family and to the world? What have you learned that will help your family to grow, to heal and to expand in *Heart*?

What is Your Story? *Write it all down* and leave it to pass on when you pass on. Let one of your gifts be to share your life lessons and *Soul* journey with those you love.

My Story - My Path of Life and Love...

_____

_____

_____

_____

_____

_____

Charity Amy Murphy

_____

_____

_____

_____

_____

_____

_____

_____

_____

_____

_____

_____

_____

_____

_____

_____

_____

_____

_____

_____

_____

_____

_____

_____

_____

_____

_____

_____

_____

(Please continue on a separate sheet or within your journal if you need to do so)

Stepping Back into Love

Completing this step marks the point of transition where you come full circle. By preparing to die (metaphorically) you are in fact learning to live. For the lessons you have learned are for you. They are also *your* gift to *your* Soul. The advice, the guidance you pass on is for you also. So, I'll ask you a question - what are you going to do with your life? What have you come here to do? What is your path back to love?

When you are finished, read what you have written, and this time take it in as you are telling yourself. Keep in mind throughout your journey that it is not how you came to be on your journey that is important; it is that you are on your journey. This is what you need to give focus to now.

Listen to your *Heart* it will lead you to your dreams. Follow it to find peace and happiness. Life is a journey in understanding love, for when we understand that we understand ourselves and who we really are.

Asserting Oneself is Knowing Oneself

Know that when you are in alignment with your *True Self* and your true path you will set your course naturally. If fear arises let it go, it is only ego, stay centered in your *Truth* and the fear will diminish. You will need not force anything, for in this state of flow you are flow itself, and you are simply following out the course that you set yourself before you came to Earth. Let all your fear go, meditate and take solitude and connect with your Truth and the Truth of your *Soul.*

The fear that surrounds the want to be assertive is as unreal as the want you think you have to be assertive. To want to be assertive is a forced/false emotion derived out of a disconnectedness with the whole Self. To assert yourself, you need to know yourself; the fear is diminished when you do because you are now speaking your *Truth* and this comes freely.

There is no assertion needed. It simply is, because you are simply you.

Opening Up Your Higher Mind

Once the true reality of *Spirit* opens within you will never experience this lifetime in exactly the same way. Facing this means letting go of fear, it means opening up to creation. It means becoming unattached to control and allowing for free fall into the reality consciousness of all existence. It means the death of ego and the stepping back into the spiritual being that you are. It is a glorious step and you will make it when you are meant to make it.

In the interim, continue to question, continue the dialogue you have started with yourself and your existence. Everyone's journey is bringing them to where they need to go. And everyone's *Soul* is guiding them on their particular path. You are always protected and looked over, you are always where you need to be, all is in divine order and you are a part of that divinity.

Allow yourself, your *True Self* to be more and more present, to be more and more real, to be more and more you. Let your Spirit shine and illuminate the world around you, and twinkle your little *Heart* out. Shine bright and keep on shining. The life of all creation is within you and you are a part of creation itself so keep growing, keep learning, keep evolving and keep moving forward in the light of your own being.

Moving Forward in Hope and Vision

Life and everyday reality as we currently know it in the western world is being held by a deeply sad and broken Spirit. Depression, apathy, hopelessness, conformism, rules, status quos and control seem to engulf our very existence. Globalization and corporate profit have become the rulers of not just companies, but of countries, societies and communities alike. We have been taught to believe in the individual as separate, as profit above people, and many people young and old are losing touch with the hope and vision they know exists deep within their Soul.

The True Freedom of Man

Capitalism was born and gave man the opportunity of free will to manifest a free life, to transcend his former life and carve out a life of choice, of hope. Out of capitalism came ownership which imprisoned the mind and body of man. The true freedom of man lies in his ability to transcend and evolve out of his own creations. To take what is for good of all and to share in love with all humanity.

It is not about this way or that, it's about taking all the best elements, truly learning, and using our accumulated knowledge of all time to manifest the future we want. A future for everyone, a future of harmony, balance, beauty and peace. It is a dream that we alone are capable of, and it starts with all of us, joining together and uniting in heart for the betterment of mankind.

The Era of Truth and Compassion

Every era has its lessons and challenges, and every era has its revolutions, its triumphs, its moments when people unite and move forward in Truth. Now is our time to move ourselves forward. To reclaim, not just our own Truth, but *Truth* itself. It is time to reconnect; it is time to move forward, it is a time to heal our world and that of all people who are here to share in the journey of life.

Let us start with healing the state of depression, hopelessness, isolation and separation that resides within the hearts and minds of young and old, male and female, and let us come together to once again unite in Spirit, in Vision and in Hope.

The Death of Ego – A New Age

The time of the new age is here, and it is an age of compassion, of love and of light.

It is a time when the human spirit is liberated from the restrictions of a life based in fear and lack. It is a time when we come home to ourselves and home to each other. The old will wash away, and the dawn will bring fresh hope.

The people of the world are transforming their selves, they are taking themselves onto the next chapter in the history of the Earth and they are doing so in a state of love and consciousness. Together, united, we lift the veil and manifest a world of Heaven here on Earth. It is the destiny of this planet to evolve and it is the destiny of human kind to be a part of that destiny.

Everyone alive here at this time came here to be a part of it. Each and all have a part to play. Each and all are in this together. We help ourselves by helping each other. We evolve together, and no one gets left behind.

The Gift of Imagination

Creation, invention and reality starts with imagination. Invention is the creation of imagination. Open up your creative power and start imagining a world of peace, a world of possibility, a world of kindness, a world of love. Let the spark of your Truth build up within you, and let it find its way out to join with all the light of all the world.

Exercise: Reality Dreaming – Imagining A World of Peace and Beauty

This exercise is like painting a picture of a world that you would love to live in, a world that fills you with wonder, delight, awe, gratitude, peace and passion. Let this be a written statement of the reality you hold in your *Heart*. A reality you envision for all humanity.

In this final step I want you to take some time and think about the reality that your *Soul* longs for. Let your *Higher Mind* open and allow it to wander and wonder through the universe, traveling across the Earth's surface taking in all the beauty and magic of life. Then take in all the dreams you have held in your *Heart* and in your *Soul* and sit with them. Let them build up inside you and take shape in your imagination. Surround them in light and watch them glow with possibility. Then simply create a space in your *Heart* and your consciousness for them to evolve into being, and *write it all down...*

My Reality for Myself and the World - As My Soul Dreams it to be...

_____

_____

_____

_____

_____

_____

_____

_____

_____

_____

_____

_____

_____

_____

_____

_____

_____

_____

_____

_____

_____

_____

_____

_____

... and so, I dreamed a dream into being.

The Alchemist is in all of Us

EPILOGUE:

Seeing the New World

Learn, grow and master the new energy.

Start creating small manifestations into form.

The new world is here, existing beneath the old one.

We can see both.

Direct your sight,

open your vision

and allow your Mind to see.

Appendix

MEDITATION:

This Moment

To Begin: Soften your eyes and clear your mind of all thought.
Bring your attention to your breath and breathe
in and out slowly and gently.
Then connect with your Body and feel yourself be more and more
in your Self, then bring yourself to this exact moment. Feel yourself
connect with your Now and still and ground yourself to the Earth
by imagining a cord of light running from the crown of your head,
down your spine and down into the Earth's core beneath your feet.

- Sit in your Space. Be in this Moment and feel yourself Present -

Then slowly, gently and softly repeat in your mind.

"This Moment"
"This Moment"
"This Moment"

Close your eyes and sit in your moment,
Stay with its peace, and breathe deeply into it.

This is your moment, your time of peace - your time for being still.
Enjoy it and use it whenever you need to come back to your Self
and bring presence to your Soul. It is all about consciousness.
Consciously be in the moment. Consciously be aware of your
consciousness, of your Source, your peace, your beauty, your light
and your love. In consciousness you are always connected. Awareness
is the key. Spirit needs time, breath, space and consciousness.

Sit within this space and allow yourself to be one with all that is.

Affirmation: I AM divinely protected at all times; I AM one with all that is.

INVOCATION

Prayer for a Healing World

I call upon all the Saints of Heaven and Earth, to manifest forth and help this Earth to heal, to help the people of the world to heal, and to transcend all illusion of limitation and separation.

I call upon all the Holy Archangels of God's creation, to assist us in our quest for healing and to manifest forth their angelic healing light, so that we can help shift our awareness up in accordance with our evolutional destiny.

I call upon all the Goddesses of love and light, truth and beauty, to manifest forth now in all planes of reality-consciousness, and to shine their healing rays of love down into our hearts so that we can awaken the spark of truth that we all hold deep within us.

I call upon all the great Kings of time inclusive to bow down their swords and lift up their hearts, to bow down their heads and lift out their arms, and to once again remember the truth of the divine feminine and reclaim their truth at her side.

I call upon all Light Workers of past, present and future to shine brightly and illuminate our path, may we all be vessels of healing light and may the healing light of the Christ vibration radiate within us all and illuminate our world, so that we all see through eyes of love.

I call upon the Ascended Masters who took the path so that we can follow. I ask them now for their guidance and teachings.

I call upon my True Self, My Soul Self to live in my Heart, to follow my Truth and fulfill my destiny.

Thank you, God, and so it is.

Namaste, Amen

Affirmation: *I AM my I AM Presence, I AM my Soul-Self-Truth.*

Notes to Self

Shambala – Takata; what is my gift to the world….

ABOUT THE AUTHOR

Charity Amy Murphy is a qualified Tera-Mai Reiki and Seichem Master; a Life and Yoga coach and a trained Therapeutic Crisis Intervention Social Care Practitioner.

Over the last twenty years she has worked extensively with adolescents and young adults, helping them to learn, develop and nurture their social and emotional selves, through building self-esteem, resilience and confidence.

Charity was born and grew up in Dublin, Ireland. She holds an Honors degree in Social and Political Science from University College Dublin and a Master's Degree in Film and Scriptwriting.

Charity runs workshops and retreats in body movement, energy awareness and personal development.

For more information please visit www.charityamymurphy.net

Also by the author: *Write it all down: Journal of Consciousness*, Balboa Press: A daily journal for developing Soul Consciousness.

Printed in the United States
By Bookmasters